KEEP 'ER LIT

Leonard Nugent

Keep 'Er Lit

Text © 2020 Leonard Nugent

Cover Design by BEAUTeBOOK

The author asserts the moral right under the Copyright, Designs and Patents Act of 1988 to be identified as the author of this work.

All Rights reserved. With the exception of brief excerpts as part of a published review, no part of this publication may be reproduced, stored in a retrieval system, or transmitted, in any form or by any means without the prior written consent of the author, nor be otherwise circulated in any form of binding or cover other than that in which it is published and without a similar condition being imposed on the subsequent purchaser.

First published April 2019

All the proceeds from this book are going directly to Open House, a charity for the homeless.

Crawley Open House has been serving the homeless and vulnerable of Crawley and West Sussex since 1994. Today they run a 26 bed high-support hostel, busy drop-in day centre open 365 days a year, three move-on houses and a community outreach team. In 2019 they managed to resettle over 60% of hostel residents to somewhere more permanent, and there were over 16,000 visits to the day centre. People come for a shower, a hot meal, to get some laundry done, to use the computer, to get some warmth & company or to see the counsellors, hair-dresser, GP or advice teams.

Crawley Open House is a UK registered charity (No. 1048919) which receives some statutory funding, but it relies heavily on the generosity of many individuals, companies, Trusts, places of worship, schools and other organisations to keep doing its vital work. For further details of their inspiring work, visit:

www.crawleyopenhouse.co.uk

CONTENTS

Preface 7
1 – Belfast 9
2 – Moving to England 21
3 – Mad for the Craic 31
4 – Early Days 43
5 – A Lucky Break 51
6 – Things are Starting to Look up 55
7 – No Committees, Please 61
8 – Getting Serious 65
9 – Deadly Sites 69
10 – Dodgy Dealing 75
11 – My Friends from Abroad 79
12 – Life's a Big Learning Curve 85
13 – Oh No, Not Again 95
14 – Investor In People 99
15 – Under the Spotlight 107
16 – The Financial Crisis 115
17 – The Island in the Sun 125
18 – 12 marathons, 12 months, 12 countries 135
19 – The Camino 143
20 – Life on the Ocean Wave 181
21 – The Starry Plough 193
22 – A Boxing Love Affair 217
23 – The Atlantic Dream 225
24 – Family and Reflections 251

PREFACE

As I sit here writing this book, in the Sunshine State of Florida, in the middle of a lockdown because of the Covid-19 pandemic, I can't help thinking about how the world has changed since I ran around the streets of Belfast as a kid all those years ago.

I've had a varied life, with lots of ups and downs over the years. All sorts of acquaintances, colleagues, and friends have told me that I should write a book.

Although I love reading, I've never had the time to write before. But this lockdown has challenged us all. It's given us all time we didn't have before. I thought I would try and salvage something positive from this once-in-a-lifetime situation.

Writing this book has not been easy. My memory isn't the greatest, but I had a lot of encouragement from Mary, and I wanted to show any young guys just starting off their business careers that anything is possible.

If this guy can do it, so can you.

My father died in December, just a few months ago. I would've loved for him to read this, because he was very proud of all his sons and daughters. I'm sure reading this book would've put a smile on his face.

I really hope you enjoy this book. I've spent many long

days and nights these last few months labouring over a keyboard. The experience has been a great learning curve.

If one person learns anything from my mistakes, this book has been a success.

— Leonard Nugent

1 | BELFAST

I was born at Belfast Mater Hospital in 1959. My Ma had six children. I was the oldest son followed by Seamus, Patrick, Michael, Celine, and Maria. Unfortunately, Michael died at a young age. We all grew up in Queen Victoria Gardens in North Belfast. In them early days, it was a very happy place to live.

Although the district was a predominantly Protestant area, and we were a Catholic family, everyone got on. All the kids played in the street together, and there was no sectarian violence then. Or at least we were shielded from it.

I remember the 12th of July every year. The streets were covered in red, white, and blue bunting to celebrate the Protestant King Billy's victory at the Battle of the Boyne. All the kids in the district joined in the celebrations. It was all good, clean, innocent fun.

Years later, unfortunately, that would all change.

Growing up in Belfast has been with me all my life. It was the best and worst of times, if you like. No one was born with a silver spoon in his mouth. I learned how to graft while at school, and the environment that my brothers and sisters and I were raised in was far from ideal. It was the beginning of the Troubles, and no one was ever safe.

Gunshots and bomb blasts were the grizzly soundtracks

of our youth. Growing up in North Belfast, I first went to Holy Family School in Newington. At age eleven, I moved on to St. Patrick's school on the Antrim Road. St. Patrick's was known as Bearnagheeha — "Barny" for short — in them days.

St. Patrick's was no ordinary school. I vividly remember British army troops walking along the corridors of the school in full army battle gear. You wouldn't have seen that scene in any other school across these islands. There was a fortified police station across the road from the school entrance, and it was almost a tradition for the lads from our school to bombard the police station with bricks, bottles, and anything else they could get their hands on.

It was no surprise that many of those kids from Bearnagheeha were involved in the Republican movement in later years.

I used to knock around with a small group at Barny. We were as thick as thieves. Our gang was Liam Davey, Joe Corner, Frankie Saunders, Tommy Donnelly, Jim McShane, and my cousin John McCloskey.

On a lot of mornings after school registration, we would all mitch off from our classes and meet up in an old haunted house further down the Antrim Road. This big old house was once the bishop's house, but in them days, it was in ruins. All the lead and copper had been stolen. We used to pull up the floorboards to light fires to keep warm. We used to stay there all day. It was great craic playing around in that big old mansion.

Other days, we headed down the Antrim Road to Carlisle Circus. All the traffic stopped at a roundabout there, and from there we used to jump onto the back of wagons. The driver never knew we were there. We would cling onto the back of those wagons for miles.

Mostly we hung around the outside of police barracks, where the wagons had to slow down to go over the speed humps. That was our chance to cling onto the back of the lorry, and off we went.

Most of the time you never knew where you were going to end up. We spent days going up and down the Falls Road or the Crumlin Road. Sometimes, you'd end up miles away out in the country. It was great craic at the time, but crazy when you think about it now.

Other days we went swimming in the Falls Baths or the Grove Baths. Some days, we went up to the waterworks and hid out there. One time, I remember we stole a load of lead from some abandoned houses at the top of Spamount Street in the New Lodge and also from the piggy at the back of the barracks on North Queen Street. We put it all together and took it to the scrap merchant.

When it came to splitting up our spoils a few days later, the others told me that the Fianna were looking for us for stealing the lead. I told the others that I didn't want my part if the Fianna were involved.

"No problem," they said. "More for us."

Kids in Belfast in them days had no fear. We had to be

fearless if we wanted to survive, because the political situation in the North of Ireland in the 70's was wild. If you grew up in Belfast, you were streetwise. Everyone was. You simply had no choice. Murder and mayhem were everywhere. It just kind of felt par for the course.

I vividly remember watching the news with my Da one night. There was a story about a riot that me and my pals had seen first-hand earlier in the day while mitching off school. Not that the old fella knew anything about that.

A lot of shooting had started in Divis Street as we were trying to get onto the back of a wagon. We ran up into Divis Flats, a vast housing complex. Divis Flats was a Republican stronghold. The Flats were a series of concrete rectangular blocks, adjoined at seemingly random angles, with balconies and covered walkways connecting individual dwellings.

When we got into the Flats, we ran along the balconies to get a better view of what was happening. When we got to the top floor, we could see all the rioting going on below us.

Out of nowhere, a guy came running along the walkway with a rifle. He dropped onto his belly. There was a gap of about 12 inches between the bottom of the balcony and the walkway. He started shooting at the army below us.

Talk about a bird's-eye view. We thought this was great. It all happened so quickly. The army started returning fire.

Ping! Ping! Ping!

The bullets ricocheted off the walls around us. I got

really scared, and we ran like the wind to the other end of the walkway to the far stairwell. I could see the soldiers charging up the stairs towards us. We shouted to the gunman that they were coming up the stairs, but he was already on his feet, swallowed up by the Flats.

***

My Ma and Da brought us all up very strict. We were taught manners and respect for our elders from an early age. I remember getting several good hidings from the old man if one of our neighbours knocked on the door complaining that one of us had been cheeky or rude. We used to get up to all sorts of mischief, as kids often do. But it was all harmless stuff, unlike a lot of today's kids.

I remember that money was always tight in our house. We never wasted anything, and times were tough, but there was always a proper dinner on our plates every night.

My Da was a merchant seaman, as many men from Belfast were at the time. He would leave the house for weeks at a time, travelling all around the world. I was always waiting for his return from a trip, whether he was in Australia, Panama, or Singapore.

Wherever he came back from, he always brought me a pennant from that country. I had dozens of them on my wall as a kid. Maybe that's where I got the bug for travelling and adventure to different countries years later.

One time, my Da was away on a trip. A bully who lived at the end of our street said something nasty to my Ma, which must have upset her. I don't know what was said, but it was not good.

I can still see it clearly now. My Da came home off the ship. After speaking to my Ma, he marched up the street to this bully's house. After knocking on the door, my Da trailed the guy out onto the street and battered him up and down the road. All the kids in the street crowded around, shouting and cheering.

It was like something out of a John Wayne movie. I don't think anything was ever said to my Ma again after that.

We all had our own chores to do every day. Mine was to clean out the fire hearth, get rid of the ashes, and light a new fire every morning before school. Even back then, I remember all the kids in the house knew how to prepare and cook dinner. It's a pity that these skills are hardly taught to youngsters today.

It must have been around the age of eight or nine that I got my first job. I used to help the milkman every weekend morning. Later in the afternoon, I would do a round with the lemonade man. I also got a paper round from Billy Duddy, who owned a paper shop in Glandore Avenue.

I never missed a morning round. Rain, snow, or hail, I was always there. Billy would often call at the house and ask if I could do someone else's round when they didn't show up.

"No problem, Billy," I'd always say.

Soon, I got to know all the rounds. I would cover all of Glandore, Seaview, Brantwood, and Fortwilliam. In them days, there was a morning delivery of the Irish News, or the Newsletter, and in the evening it was the Belfast Telegraph.

Most evenings, after doing my own round, I would go around the other paperboys rounds. I knew the letter-boxes that you could not get the paper all the way in, so I would take it in turns, a different round every night. I'd take the papers back out of the letterboxes and I'd sell these in the local pubs. If Billy had any papers left at the end of the night, I took them. I would head for the Somerton Inn Pub or along the Antrim Road to the Phoenix Pub, selling the extras.

I used to love to give my Ma the money every week. It was a great feeling. These early days shaped my enthusiasm for a pound note!

Around that time, my Ma took Seamus and me to join the St. John Bosco boxing club down by the co-op in Belfast. All the boys in my family have had a love affair with boxing to this very day.

In the early days, the old man used to make up a sort of a ring in our back entry. He would tie socks around our hands for gloves. We would then batter each other's heads off with these socks as gloves for hours on end. Other kids from the street would also join in as well. It was great craic, and it certainly taught us how to look after ourselves from that early age.

Learning how to box was such an important part of my childhood. Boxing remains a key component of my life to this very day. All our family hate bullies. My Da made sure we understood the need to stick up for ourselves. If we came home from school with a black eye, our parents would always ask how we got it. If the response wasn't the right one, you could expect a matching shiner on the other eye.

In between ships, my Da found it very hard to find work, as most Catholic men did in Belfast in them times. With a name like Seamus, it was obvious to any new employer he was a Catholic. He did find the occasional gig as a barman, working in the Christian Brothers Club on the Antrim Road. He also worked at Hayloft Bar in central Belfast before it was blew up. When opportunities in Belfast dried up around 1971, he left for England to find work on the construction sites around Crawley in Sussex, where my uncle Leonard — also known as "Cracknose" — lived.

My Da would send home money every week to my Ma. It must have been very hard for her during those times, with five growing kids to look after.

Every other evening, my Ma and I would walk for miles to find a public phone box that worked so she could ring my Da in England. In our area, you had no chance, but if you walked to the better middle class areas, you would find a working phone box.

Sometimes, there could be a curfew in West Belfast, and the night would be deadly quiet. We would hear the odd gun battle going on, or hear an explosion filling the night air. The noise never seemed far away, so we almost always ran to get home as quickly as possible.

Belfast was changing fast. Most of the Catholic families in our area were moving out, as it wasn't safe anymore. We stopped going to the 12th of July marches, and we tended to only play with the Catholic kids left in the area.

One night while we were all in the house, a large group of Protestants turned up outside the house shouting sectarian slogans. We thought we were going to get burnt out that night.

My Ma was upstairs getting the young ones dressed quickly, gathering some clothes and getting downstairs. I was at the back door trying to open it, but the snib that slid across to open the door had broken. Panicking, I was scrambling about trying to find a nail to use instead of the snib to open the door. In the end, I got it open and we all headed into our back entry to escape. Luckily, the police or army turned up and the crowd disappeared.

After that, the writing was on the wall for us. We would have to leave the area.

Not long after, my Da was back in Belfast. Our house was raided late at night by the British army. They told us that they had received a report that a gunman had been seen on our roof. So they wrecked the house looking for this supposed gunman.

It was all total rubbish, part of the intimidation process

that a lot of Catholics faced in those times. It was also the straw that broke the camel's back. My Ma and Da decided the best thing to keep us all safe was to move to England.

Butter wouldn't melt!

My Ma & Da, late fifties, with his young sisters

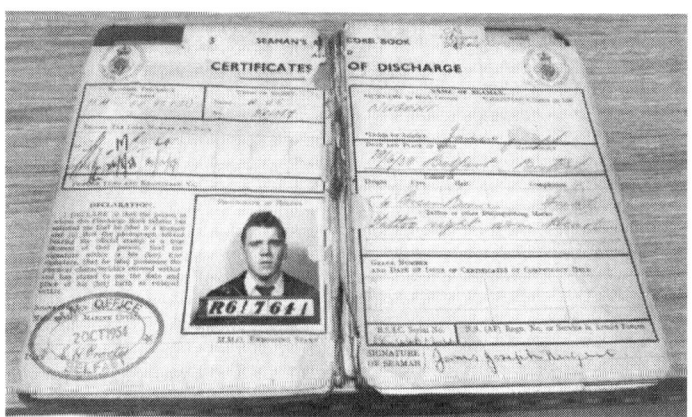
The old man's discharge book from the navy

Me, Seamus & Paddy at my Aunt Margaret's wedding in Belfast

2 | MOVING TO ENGLAND

Belfast Refugees Come to Crawley was the headline. A few weeks earlier, the Nugents had been on the move. Our whole family moved to England in 1973. We ended up in Crawley, a town just south of London

We had to get away from the harsh, violent environment in our native Northern Ireland. The old man had been struggling to put food on our table. The Troubles were all the rage in the UK media, so the Crawley newspaper did a piece about us moving there. The local council would not re-house us, so the old man took us all down to the steps of the local council and told the newspapers about our struggle.

At first, the local authority wanted to split us all up into different institutions. But the old man wasn't having that. His ploy with the newspapers did the trick. After a short period in sheltered accommodation, the council found us a home in Langley Green.

At last, we began to live a normal life. Even if we were getting some funny looks around the town from the locals who'd seen our story in the paper.

I had two years left of school to finish, but the new surroundings — St Wilfrid's School — didn't ignite a sudden love of learning. I made some good pals: Kim and Lee Burrows, Vince Hooper, Dave Whelan, Mike Kennedy,

Joey Bent, Chris Digan, Simon Newell, Eric Minogue and Robert Butler.

One day while bunking off classes, I noticed a hatch in the roof of the boys toilet.

"What's up there?" I thought.

Someone gave me a leg up and I climbed up into the loft space above the boys toilet.

"It's dark up here!" I shouted down. "Someone throw me up some matches."

With a lighted match, I was able to find a light bulb. We had found a new den to hide away from classes in.

After a week of about five of us using the new hideaway, someone started to smoke. I hated smoking — still do. So I moved along the rafters of the roof to get away from the smoke.

Next thing I knew, I was falling between the rafters into a geography class below! The teacher and the kids in the class couldn't believe it. One minute they were all looking at the blackboard. The next I was falling through the ceiling. I took a caning from the headmaster and a massive bollocking from my Ma for that one.

Another escapade that earned me a caning was taking Mr. Weaver's car. With about ten kids, we pushed his car from the staff car park across the school's football pitches and into a lake. Mr. Weaver had apparently hit one of the girls in our year — Ann Giles, I think — and this was his payback. The car ended up in the water about ten feet down an embankment. Another bollocking...

During lunchtime, some of us would take off our school ties and try our luck at getting served in the Swan Pub near the school. Some of the older-looking kids had no problem at all in getting served.

Inside the Swan, there used to be a small snug we all headed for. Whoever was getting served passed the beers back to us. We didn't have a lot of time, so after a quick light and bitter it was back to school.

I used to fall asleep at the back of the class. The teacher had no idea we would be half cut. I don't suppose that could happen these days.

In truth, though, I bloody hated school. I was always bunking off and ended up taking no exams. Yet Crawley was the perfect place for us. It was a green and white home away from home.

There were Irish everywhere you looked, mainly from the west of Ireland. So fitting in wasn't a problem or a hardship. I quickly discovered my own kind of haven: Crawley Amateur Boxing Club, where the likes of former world middleweight champ Alan Minter learned the ropes. Seamus and I joined the club with Frankie Lyons around 1974.

It wasn't long before the work ethic that my Ma and Da had instilled in us came to the fore. I was about fifteen when I started working at Pepe's Golden Griddle on Crawley High Street. Pepe's was a local fast food joint that gave me more than I ever could have hoped for.

The owner — yeah, you've guessed it, Pepe — was a massive influence on me. He was a bit of a playboy and told me about all these scrapes he got himself into in his younger days. Crazy stories of fast cars and faster women were just what a wide-eyed lad wanted to hear. But his true message was stark, and it stuck with me.

"Work, work, work," he said. "Of course, have a beer, chase ladies, do whatever you want. But the bedrock to anything has to be hard graft. Work, and the success will come."

I'd love to have a chat with him now. He doesn't have a clue about my journey, or how his pep talks about coming over from Spain without a pot to piss in inspired me.

At the same time, I picked up a paper round and carried on pulling off the kind of strokes which served me so well in Belfast. Seamus and I started a cut and shut bicycle business, stealing bikes from everywhere, chopping and changing them up before selling to any interested folk. Good fun for a while... until we got caught.

Initially, I wanted to be a chef. So I enrolled at Crawley College to do a City and Guilds catering course. I enjoyed it, but started cooking up trouble rather than tasty dinners. At just sixteen, I ended up in prison for fighting for the first time. I finished up my City and Guild certificates in jail.

Unfortunately, this experience wasn't an unlucky one-off.

Feltham Young Offenders was an awful place. It was predominantly full of young black lads. This fact was so noticeable, and I always wondered why.

Back then the Stop and Search laws preyed on the black communities, and the Police were ruthless in taking them to task. Most of them had done nothing more than being pulled up by the Old Bill. This didn't sit right with me. It opened my eyes to what can happen in the justice system.

Being locked up 23 hours a day definitely took some getting used to. The noise was just unbelievable. A lot of these lads had never been away from their families. At night, you heard a lot of crying and shouting. It was a really violent place, but I wasn't worried about looking after myself. I just had to tune in mentally to cope.

I was scared, but not as bad as some others in there. Why? I had a secret weapon with me. It was in my back pocket and only came out when it was needed.

My red mist trigger kept me alive in and outside of the nick. Once the alarm bells sounded, I just crossed over. All of a sudden, I just didn't care. That was my backup to help me deal with situations. It was a Belfast thing I think, but it got me out of many a scrape.

A lot of rows inside the nick were over stupid, trivial stuff like cigarettes or drugs. The currency inside was tobacco. I never smoked, so there was no personal need to go looking for anything or borrow to get my fix. I never needed favours from anyone. The only chance you got to settle some scores with people and have a fight was during the one hour of 'exercise,' when you could finally spend some time outside.

Grim times indeed.

Feltham Young Offenders is about 60 miles from Crawley. This was before the M25, so when the old man came down to see me, he took a Honda 50 motorbike. Nice idea, but it took him six hours to get there through all the backroads from Crawley. Today, you'd be there in 40 minutes.

"I won't be coming here again," or words to that effect, he grumbled when he saw me.

Wish I could have said the same.

After coming out of Feltham I started working with the old man on the building of the new Hilton hotel at Gatwick, he got me the start as an apprentice scaffolder. After a few months I found I was arguing with the old man all the time on the site. It wasn't working out. So one Friday as soon as I got my wages about £80 in them days I walked into the airport, bought a ticket, and ended up in Dublin that night, I never told anyone, I thought I would get a job in construction no problem.

In them days, all the construction sites in Dublin were run by the unions and you needed to be in the know, which I wasn't, there was also a recession in Ireland at that time and as I walked around the streets of Dublin day after day, going from site to site, I started to get delusion with the whole place, no one would give me a chance.

The £80 I had on the Friday was long gone and I was sleeping in a homeless shelter and stealing food from supermarkets, after nearly two weeks of trying to find work I went to the UK embassy to see if they would give me the money for the flight back to England, they wouldn't give me the funds for the ticket, but told me I could use the embassy phone to get someone in England to buy me a ticket.

This was long before mobile phones and, in fact, my Ma or Da never had a phone in the house either. In an emergency we could use our neighbors phone, and so in desperation I rung the neighbor and asked could she go next door to my Ma house, I explained to my Ma that I was in Dublin, I had no money, and could she arrange to buy me a ticket.

It was with a sheepish grin on my face that I turned up a few days later back in Crawley to face a massive bollocking from the old man. That whole episode taught me a lot, but mostly about what homeless people go through and I have a lot of empathy and understanding with them to this day.

Ma, Da, Me, Granny McCrory, Celine & Maria, my sisters. 1975

Leonard Nugent

Front page news

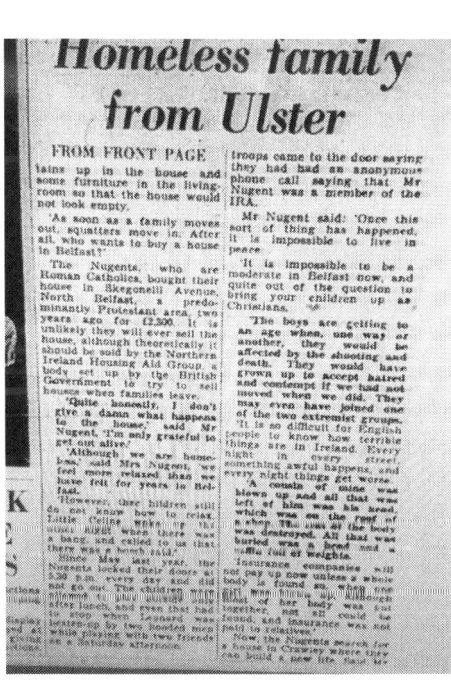

Just arrived in England

At school in England, that's our Seamus to my right

*1974, Littlehampton,
with Ma, Da, Aunt Margaret & our sisters Celine & Maria*

3 | MAD FOR THE CRAIC

In the early 80s, I got involved in the whole Rockabilly scene. We had a gang going to London three or four nights a week, bunking the train from Gatwick to Victoria, then bunking the admission to the clubs where we could.

We had next to nothing and a very carefree attitude. There were nine or ten of us, mostly English lads from Crawley and Horley. Seamus and I were on the rampage every weekend and loved every minute. Whether we went to clubs in London or weekenders in Great Yarmouth, we had great craic. One of the bands, The Flying Saucers, even paid us a few quid to start a fight one night so they could include it in their new video.

The scraps were memorable too. Skinheads, football fans, Teddy boys, and other Rockabilly gangs all fancied a piece of action. We were out most nights causing havoc. But if you weren't in by 11 pm, the old man locked the door.

"This is my house, and you will follow my rules," he would tell us. Not that we listened. We had an outside toilet, so my Ma left a blanket on top of the cistern. My bed for the night was often the stone cold floor.

I say "night," but we would often get a 4 am post train from London to Three Bridges and then walk home. We'd sleep in the outside bog for a couple hours before the old man came knocking on the toilet door at 6:30am to get us ready for work. I spent countless nights sleeping in there, but we never missed a shift from work.

Other nights, we would throw small pebbles up at our Paddy's bedroom window, and he would quietly slip down the stairs and let us in the back door.

My parents had settled well in England. The only trouble came when the police arrived if me or my brother had been fighting. Eventually, my wayward lifestyle became too much, and the old man kicked me out. I ended up living with my Uncle Cracknose.

Living with my uncle, the drinking and singalongs were endless, but one day really sticks in my mind. I came back to my uncle's house from the site. We had been rained off. I heard all this Irish music playing as soon as I got out of the van. Nothing unusual in that. There were always parties in the house.

But what wasn't normal was a prosthetic leg lying in the hallway. A pair of pants, too. Old Cracknose had pulled a one-legged bird. In the rush for romance, something fell off.

"There's a leg on the floor," I shouted up the stairs to him and his new friend, not knowing it was hers.

"Yeah, we know!" The joint response came from the lovebirds. That kind of craziness was normal.

Fighting, drinking, being a pest with the Rockabilly boys. Those were the days. I was always working, though, and never missed a day of grafting. Balance is — and always will be — key. Have your fun. But do your work. That was the work ethic the old man had drilled into us.

One night after leaving a Rockabilly club in East London, a few of us got into a bit of a scrape with some skinheads on the last tube of the night. There was a massive brawl, and at the end of it, one of our guys — Steve Gregory — had been stabbed a few times.

In all the scrapes that we had been involved in, only fists were used, never weapons. This was the first time this had happened.

Soon, the tube line was shut down, and the Old Bill were everywhere. We all ran in different directions. Steve ended up in hospital. To cut a long story short, I ended up in the dock of the local magistrates' court.

The old magistrate was having none of my blarney about what happened. He gave me three months detention. He called the punishment a "short, sharp shock."

I ended up in a detention centre in Kent called HMP Blantyre House. The idea of this place was to teach young offenders army-style discipline to keep them from a life of crime.

The day started at 6 am with drills. You marched everywhere, no walking. There were drills and marching all day long in between work and physical education. I was never as fit in my life as when I was in there.

After assessment, I applied to work in the kitchen. Since I had already been to catering college and had worked in some kitchens, that's where they sent me. I kept my head down. Thanks to my experience, I was soon number two in the kitchen. This brought a lot of perks and got me out of a lot of the marching and drills. It also meant I was never hungry.

Most of the lads worked all day out on the prison farms, and the screws never made it easy for them. Instead of using tractors, the inmates were made to do everything by hand. In the winter months, it was freezing out there. When they came in at night, they had to do more marching and drills before they got any dinner. So everyone was always hungry.

We slept in dormitories, with about 30 lads in each one. As soon as the lights went out every night at 9 pm and the screws left, all sorts of scores were settled.

Saturday was the only time you could have visitors. Most of the lads there used to smuggle things in. You were allowed to have a pot of tea during your visit, and when the teapots came back to us in the kitchen, we retrieved what was being smuggled. It was mainly tobacco.

This was a great perk for the number one and number two in the kitchen, as we took our cut from everything that passed through the kitchen. I never smoked, so I always bartered, ending up with a huge stash of sweets and toiletries.

Two friends from Crawley — Christy O'Shea and Steve Whelan — also came to the Blantyre House while I was there. Steve was a very good friend of my brother Seamus, and I looked after him very well from the kitchen. Christy spent a lot of time in the prison hospital. It could be very hard in that tough environment, especially with everyone trying to prove themselves all the time.

It was tough to see the attempted suicides and the mental struggles in the house. I knew people who took their own lives. The disturbing, unsettling film *Scum* — starring a very young Ray Winstone — about life inside back then was sadly bang on.

Did I come out reinvigorated and reformed? No. I came out as fit as a fiddle and learned a few lessons. But I was soon back in the Rockabilly scene.

We used to visit clubs all over London in those days. The St Hillier Arms in Carshalton, Bumbles in Wood Green, The Royalty in Southgate, The Swan at the Oval, The Telegraph at the top of Brixton Hill, and many others. My mates then were Mark and Jeff Stuart, John Corrigan, Steve Gregory, Pat Mooney, Radar, and Seamus. Mostly, it was just the music we loved, and dressing in that southern redneck style. We were following bands like Ray Campi, Mac Curtis, Crazy Cavern, Matchbox, and The Flying Saucers. We followed these bands all over the place.

Only a few months after coming out of HMP Blantyre, I was having a pint in Crawley High Street with some friends. When I was walking between pubs, a copper called me over. He knew I had been away and started making abusive remarks.

I bit, of course. That was probably his ploy all along. Next thing, we were both rolling around on the floor punching each other in the head. Within minutes, a police van turned up, and I was on my way to Crawley nick.

Once we arrived at the police station, I was bundled into a cell with about five coppers kicking lumps out of me. I ended up naked and handcuffed on the floor. I stayed that way for most of the night. I couldn't go to the toilet. Every part of me ached, and my face was like the Elephant Man.

I should have ignored the copper that night and kept my mouth shut. But that was how I used to be. In the morning, they charged me with assault on the copper.

I couldn't believe it. I looked like I had been in a traffic accident, and they charged me. I eventually made my way home. My Granny Nugent, who was staying with us that week from Belfast, opened the door and let out a squeal.

"Jesus Christ! What happened?"

I explained to her and my Ma, and they took me straight to Crawley Hospital.

The doctors wanted to know what happened. After taking x-rays, they did a report listing all the bruises, cuts, and lacerations. When the old man came home from work, he went straight to the Crawley police station and kicked up. We also made a complaint to the Police Complaints Board. One night, after months of seemingly nothing happening, a chief inspector turned up at the house.

"Sorry," he told us. "There isn't enough evidence to

charge any police officers."

We couldn't believe it. We had taken photos of all the injuries. We had the doctor's photos, reports, and assessments, and still they said there wasn't enough evidence. The old man grabbed the inspector by the collar and showed him the front door.

I was wrong that night, undoubtedly. But the police should never be allowed to get away with these things. I think this was where I gained a healthy disrespect for the law.

Apart from this tangle with the police, everything else was going great. This was the early 1980s. I was training at the boxing club a couple of times a week and working on the hod carrying bricks all day long.

I met Ricky Masterson one night in the Fox Pub. We became great friends. He was the best man at my wedding years later. Ricky and I worked together as hod carriers for a while. Eventually, we moved into digs with some other friends.

You can imagine the craic. Ricky and I lived with Dave and Ray Todd, two brothers from Manchester who were both steel fixers. We were four young guys, and we had a great time at 2 Spencer's Road in Crawley. And if them walls could speak, they would tell you a great story.

At the end of every week, I used to cook a big stew for us all. We had a massive pot that took up all four of the burners on the stove. After putting all the meat and veg into the pot,

I would go through the cupboards to see whatever else was left. It all went into the pot, cooking for around 5-6 hours. A big lovely stew, and it did us nearly all week. We would come in from the site at night, or the pub, and just light the burner under the pot. Great stuff!

In those days, the pubs had different hours of operation. They used to close at 2:30 in the afternoon. During the week, we never missed work. But at the weekends, it wasn't uncommon to end up with a carry-out back to the digs for a singsong once the Fox shut.

Back then, there seemed to be so many more characters around than today. And the Fox had more than its fair share of characters. Belfast Jimmy, Mick Molloy, PJ McHale, Dublin Chris, Jimmy the Muck, Jamie Webster Johnny and Kevin O'Hara. Almost to a man, they were all building workers. The craic was unbelievable. The pubs today just aren't the same. It was a sad day when the Fox closed its doors for the last time to make way for a new road.

One day, Ricky asked me to go to Magaluf for a week's holiday. I had never been abroad before. I didn't have to think about it.

"Count me in," I said.

A few weeks later, we were leaving Gatwick heading for Spain. I didn't know what to expect, but had read all the papers and the stories of the antics that went on there and couldn't wait to see for myself.

After arriving and checking into the hotel we went

straight to the bar. We couldn't believe how cheap it was, and the craic was 90. After trying out a few bars, we ended up in a right dive with the music blaring.

"Two pints, please, mate," I told the barman.

We had only just sat down when a row had started, nothing to do with us. Within minutes, the Spanish police were on the scene, and they were taking no prisoners. Ricky and I got split up in all the confusion, and next thing I knew I was in a police wagon on the way to the station.

I couldn't believe my luck. Only in the country a few hours and already in the nick. But this place was a whole different story than the UK. I ended up in there for a week before they deported me.

This place was like something out of Midnight Express. About 30 of us were in the cell together. No one spoke English, and they were mostly in there for drug offences. The embassy guy came but was no real help. He was the only English person that I spoke to.

Every day, they gave out a loaf of black bread and a bottle of water. One day, they came and took me out.

"Great," I thought. "I'm going home."

They brought me back to the hotel to get my suitcase. Ricky was at the hotel and tried to talk to me, but the guards weren't having it. The sun was blistering, and I could see everyone playing in the swimming pool. But I was back in the police van heading back to the nick. I was gutted.

I didn't sleep a wink in that place. I was too scared. I kept my back to the wall all day. In a strange way, I was lucky that I had experienced this sort of thing before. I had an inner strength to hold onto.

It was a big relief after a week to be escorted back to the airport in handcuffs and put on a plane. The other people on the plane must have thought I was one of the great train robbers. It just goes to show how innocently being in the wrong place at the wrong time can make such a difference. It was a nightmare, but this was the kind of character-building stuff you can't get by reading a self-help book from a Buddhist guru.

That said, I still wasn't having any moments of clarity. No realizations that I could, perhaps, be screwing up my life. I was only 24 years old.

But perhaps the penny was slowly starting to drop, as I had met a girl. I didn't want to carry on in the same way.

Leonard Nugent

Rockabilly days

That's when I had hair!, some of the gang

4 | EARLY DAYS

The boys carried on living in the digs, but I needed out, so I moved into a room in the Barrington Hotel. Sadly, in retrospect, it was the right call. Dave and Ray, two of the other lads I lived with, ended up drinking themselves to death.

Being surrounded by so many Irish families helped us settle in England, but there were some seriously frustrating drawbacks. All the contractors in and around Crawley were Irish. It was like the Mafia. Everyone was from the West of Ireland, so if you hailed from the "Black North" as they called it or Dublin, it was a problem. The Culchies, as we called them, wouldn't give us Belfast lads any work. They only looked after their own townies, so we would have to travel up to 30 odd miles away to earn our corn despite so much happening on our doorstep.

A few years later, I was able to win a lot of local construction contracts. And how I loved that! A Belfast boy was picking up all the local work and putting the green-eyed monster from the West of Ireland's nose out of joint.

After many years, I was an overnight success and my vans were all over the place.

"Who the hell is this Nugent fella?" Everyone asked.

It took me twenty years to get to that stage, though. Not

that anyone else realized it.

The room in the Barrington Hotel wasn't the best, but I asked my girlfriend Zoe to move in with me. After a few months living in cramped conditions, I decided I wouldn't carry on living like this.

After some soul searching, I eventually 'copped myself on' and asked Zoe to marry me. She said yes. That was my incentive to do something about my whole situation. Between us, we decided to buy our own house and start a family.

I knocked the whole pub scene on the head right away. I couldn't afford it anymore. I set myself a target of raising and saving the £30,000 deposit that I would need for a mortgage within the next year. It was a massive undertaking, but with both of us working, no socializing, and me ducking and diving, I had no doubt we would raise the funds.

I was still struggling to get work locally because of my Belfast background. Finally, I managed to get a start with an Irish company called CravenStar, who had a contract with British Rail, laying concrete troughs to hold cables at the side of the track. Most of the work was on the track between London and Brighton.

I worked on a gang with Belfast Jimmy, Tommy Ryan, and Peter Doyle. These guys were all a lot older than me, and I learned a lot from all of them. The craic was mighty. Our work was mostly shoveling track ballast all day long and laying the concrete troughs.

There were also night shifts involved and I put myself up for every night shift I could. The night shift did not start until 10 pm and lasted until British rail took possession of the track around 4 am. The morning shift started at 8 am.

It seemed impossible for someone to work both the day shift and the night shift, but we would only probably work for about an hour on the night shift. Then we got some sleep in one of the old rail carriages or nipped back to our old transit van for a kip.

After a few months of doing the day and night shifts, I was saving good money. But I could see I wasn't going to hit my target of £30,000. Zoe was working all the shifts the Penta Hotel would give her, but it still wasn't enough.

So I went and saw my old mate, Pepe, at the Golden Griddle and asked if I could work in his place from 6 pm till about 9.30pm cooking on the grill. He was glad to see me back. On paper, I was now working 24 hours a day. There's no way a person's body could work all them hours. But I wasn't working them — I was getting paid for them. The lads in the gang were very good to me. They all knew what I was trying to do, so during the day they would cover for me while I went for a kip in the back of the transit van.

To try and save up £30,000 in a year seemed inconceivable, but it wasn't impossible. It was a really big ask, but I knew I would do it because I had given myself a target, and having that to focus on made it easier. I was so determined. It taught me a lot about myself and how far I could push myself.

After twelve months, we had the full £30,000. I also had the satisfaction of knowing that I had given myself a target and had achieved it.

"Nothing will stop me now," I thought.

In 1984, at the age of 24, I bought our first house.

At the end of 1984, I was approached by MJ Mansell, who at that time were one of the largest groundwork contractors in the Southeast of England. They wanted me to be their foreman on a large housing contract in Crowborough in Sussex.

I said I'd do it, but I wanted to bring the gang from CravenStar with me. This was my first proper job as a foreman, and all the guys on the site were a lot older and more experienced than me. This was a very tough task, and it took me a while to earn everyone's respect. But I was a quick learner and I pushed everyone very hard, sometimes too hard. I was eager to prove myself.

Once a week, the surveyor for MJ Mansell came to the site to measure the work we had done in the previous week. His name was John Brown, and we became good friends. I was always picking John's brain about surveying. I was eager to learn everything from him — what parts of the contract made money and what parts didn't, etc.

As the site progressed, I was starting to understand the financial side of construction very well. John became ill for a few weeks, and another surveyor from Mansell's main office turned up to take over. His name was Mark Schneidau.

I didn't know it then, and neither did Mark, but we would end up working with each other for the next 30 odd years. Mark has been a big influence on me, and I think I've had a big influence on him as well. We've worked well with each other and have never had a cross word in all them years, something I'm very proud of.

As I mentioned before, my Ma and Da had always instilled in all us kids that work ethic. I had just proved to myself that with a lot of hard work and determination, you could achieve anything you wanted.

So I went out and bought a lorry and started a small business with my friend Ricky. We would go and knock on doors, giving people quotes for a new driveway or patio. We would clear rubbish from gardens, cut down trees, and do anything where we could make a few pounds.

My old friend Tommy McLaughlin (Irish Tommy) gave us advice and guidance. We couldn't always afford to fix the lorry when it broke down, so Tommy would help us. The lorry never seemed to be out of Tommy's garage in them early days.

After coming to England, I was very lucky to have met Tommy, a man who had the same spirit as myself. He and his wife Audrey have become great family friends. In fact, Tommy and Audrey are godparents to my daughters, Faye and Sinead, and have been very good to both of them. I learned a lot from Tommy. He had been around the block once or twice and was always there with good advice and encouragement.

Unfortunately, Tommy died in 2018 from cancer. That was a big loss to us allAfter a year or so of my partnership with Ricky, I decided to go it alone. Some partnerships work, but I was very focused. I wanted to do things my own way, so we both decided to try something new.

Zoe and I got married in 1985. About a year or so later, Faye, our first daughter, was born. What a feeling that was!

Zoe had a cancer scare during the pregnancy and dealt with it really well. Now with a daughter to look after, I was taking no prisoners. I was determined to make my new business a success. I bought a new lorry and started my brother Paddy on the payroll. Soon, we had another lorry on the road and took on another few workers. Almost all of the work at the time was cash, which was great, but it could also be a problem. I realized I needed an accountant.

Preferably one who saw paying Her Majesty's tax the same way I did.

Having Paddy on board was great. He had the same values as me, and I didn't need to explain too much to him. He worked the men like it was his own business.

My Ma used to do a cleaning job at night for Eddie McMullan, a friend of the family who operated a freight forwarding business out of Gatwick. Eddie mostly moved racehorses to different countries for rich clients. While my Ma was cleaning the offices, my Da would use the company's copier to print off hundreds of flyers that I had designed.

Every night after dinner, Zoe and I would go up and down the streets of Crawley, putting these flyers through the doors of every house. We wouldn't stop until every flyer was posted. She would be pushing the pram with Faye inside going up one side of the street, while I was jumping over the hedges on the other side of the street.

That was how we got most of our work at the start. Later, we got a lot of work by word of mouth and recommendations.

With my great friend, Irish Tommy.

5 | A LUCKY BREAK

After a few years of building up the business, I realized that in the long term, to really do things properly, I would need to be a lot more professional. I would need to move away from cash-in-hand operations.

I started by writing letters to the bigger national contractors offering our services. After writing hundreds of letters, I realized that I would be very lucky to get in the door this way. I changed my focus to local contractors. Even this strategy proved fruitless. I usually didn't even receive an acknowledgment of the letters I sent.

But I couldn't give up. So I went to the regional offices of the main contractors and started knocking on their doors. This was before company websites, so it was hard to find out who was even the right person to ask for. I usually went to the reception desk and blagged my way in. I would ask a question, see what answer I got, and go from there.

Sometimes, I got to see someone. Sometimes, I got shown the door.

I traveled all around the southeast of England knocking on prospective clients' doors. It was very exhausting and demoralizing, but I couldn't give up.

One day, I received a call from Bob Moran, the director at Rydon Construction. One of my letters had come across his desk, and he must have liked my ambition or my cheek. He invited me to their head office for an interview. I couldn't believe it — after all the letters I had sent, all the miles I had traveled, someone was giving me a chance. So off I went suited and booted and tried to sell my wares to Rydon Construction.

I knew during the interview it was going well. Sometimes you can just tell. I told Bob what he wanted to hear and was punching well above my weight. He asked that I come back for a second interview in a few days' time.

This time, Bob had Chris Stevens, his surveying director, with him. After interrogating me for around 30 minutes, they offered me a contract for the groundworks on a large block of flats at Burnt Ash Hill near Hither Green in South London. They gave me the contract to take away and look at. If I agreed to the contract, I would start in three weeks.

I read the contract and was very happy. But what did I know about contracts? So I showed it to the old man.

"Don't trust them fuckers," he muttered after reading it.

But I had met Bob and Chris, and my instinct was that I could trust them. Also, the payment terms were fortnightly, which would help my cashflow. So I signed the contract and sent it back.

A week or so later, there was a pre-start meeting in Rydon's office. Things were moving very quickly. I had never been in any sort of meeting before. I tried to hide that fact by showing confidence and a "can-do" attitude.

They gave me the construction programme. The work had to be done in sixteen weeks. I told them I would be finished long before sixteen weeks. I don't think they believed me, but they were smiling, and off I went.

I still had Paddy and the boys working with the lorries carrying out the driveways, patios, and crossover works. I wanted to keep that going just in case a problem came up with the Rydon contract. Although I knew I couldn't keep doing the cash-in-hand projects, it was very hard to give that up.

Taking on this contract also brought a lot more responsibility. Suddenly, I had to think about employers and third-party liability insurance, tax, VAT, transportation for getting the men to work, etc. It was a massive learning curve, but I was like a sponge soaking everything up, learning new things every day. I invested £25,000 in a secondhand excavator, a Liebherr 912. Over the years, I worked that old girl nearly every daylight hour.

After starting this first contract for Rydon's, we worked seven days a week. I was still going out at night with Zoe posting the flyers in the letterboxes of Crawley for Paddy's side of the business. I had so much energy that there weren't enough hours in the day for me.

Part of the contract required that I go out into the main road of a London bus route to connect a new main sewer to the new development. I was meant to liaise with the local authority, and their inspector was supposed to supervise the process.

Because of bureaucratic red tape at the local authority, they would never answer my letters or phone calls. I had almost finished the contract well before the sixteen weeks were up, but these buggers at the council were going to make me look bad because I couldn't arrange the new sewer connection. All the hard graft we had put in would be for nothing. So I just ignored them. I made the connection into the main road, forged the inspectors signature, and kept my mouth shut.

Rydon was over the moon. They were impressed that I had finished the project way ahead of schedule. They called me into their office again to look at another contract.

With my brothers, Seamus & Paddy

6 | THINGS ARE STARTING TO LOOK UP

After successfully completing the first contract for Rydon, they gave me another contract in Windsor, not far from the castle. The contract was for a development of twenty new houses. Once again, I finished ahead of schedule.

Next, they asked me to look at a new project in Woolwich. This was the big league — around 100 new homes. By this time, I was now employing around 25 guys. I had stopped all the cash-in-hand works around Crawley, but I had also now attracted the attention of other main contractors. I was getting offers to tender for new contracts all around the southeast.

The name was starting to grow because I had a lot of name boards made up. These were three feet x three feet white fluted boards with our name and contact details. I put them up all over South London, Sussex, Surrey, and Kent. I used to put them on old derelict sites belonging to other people. It looked as if we had the contract, when of course we didn't. But it gave the impression that we were a much bigger company than we were. I was punching well above my weight.

The Woolwich contract was daunting to me at first. I had never taken on a project of this size before. But I had so much self-belief and enthusiasm, I knew I could pull it off.

Doubts would cross my mind the odd time at night when I was sitting at home, but these thoughts never lasted too long.

When we started that contract, I had to employ a lot more guys. Some of them guys are still with the company today 30 years later. Young Richard Webster started with us here on this contract with his dad, and I'm glad to say Richard is still with the company today.

At the same time, I had started a contract in Crawley for a local company called Gorringe. I was constructing the new roads and horse stables for the estate of Paolo Gucci (of Gucci fame).

After a few months, Gorringe stopped my payments under some made-up story of bad workmanship. I tried to reason with them. I was eventually told the real reason for the non-payment: Gucci had stopped paying them, so they couldn't pay me.

I wasn't having that, so I dug a trench across the site's entrance with an excavator so no one could enter or leave the site. Soon enough, Penny, a lady from the Gucci office, came to see me. I had gotten to know her over the course of the contract, in fact not long after she married Gucci.

She asked what I was doing, I told her that I wasn't being paid for all my previous work. I explained that I had been accused of bad workmanship, and now I was being told that because Gucci would not pay Gorringe, Gorringe would not pay me.

"Come with me," she said. She took me into Paolo Gucci's office and asked me to explain again what I had told her.

He was furious. He asked me what I was owed and wrote me a cheque then and there. He also asked me to take over the whole contract from Gorringe.

This wasn't the last time that I had to use the digger to blockade a site. Sometimes, you had to think outside the box to ensure you got paid.

***

In October 1987, we had the Great Storm. The whole southeast of England was like a battlefield. Millions of trees were down, and properties were wrecked everywhere. Winds of over 130 miles per hour had devastated the landscape.

"This is a great opportunity," I thought. Builders were required everywhere, and you could set your own price for everything.

The government also passed the Special Powers Act, which allowed you to run on red diesel during this period. We seized that opportunity, although I only had a few lorries.

I was approached by an Irish friend, PJ McHale, to take on a contract with the West Sussex County Council. I would remove all the fallen trees across the county, load them onto wagons, and bring them to the burning site at Ardingly

Show Grounds, where they had permanent bonfires going 24/7 for months to get rid of all the trees.

To fulfill the contract, I needed to buy more wagons. The problem was that there was such a short supply of wagons for sale because of all the work. In the end, I scrounged up wagons from all over the place. They were real old dogs, with no lights or windows and cracked windscreens. Certainly, no tax or insurance. They ran on the red stuff also.

Every day, we were getting police escorts, as the trees we were removing from the roads and footpaths were of all shapes and sizes. The police never made a comment about the wrecks that we were using. This was an emergency, and whatever was needed to get the roads and paths open was no problem.

In the days after the storm, I approached several timber mills and agreed a price for the supply of oak trees. Initially, I didn't know what oak looked like, but I soon learned. So instead of removing all the fallen trees — as our contract stipulated — our gangs started cutting down the oak trees. The bigger, the better.

We would set up mobile traffic lights, putting them both on red so that no cars would come through and see what we were doing. The police escorts were usually sitting there watching us, not knowing what was going on. We would pick the biggest oaks that we could find, cut them down, and head straight to the timber mills to get paid. We had a good run at this, but in the end the price of oak went down, as there was just so much about.

Months later, at the end of the contract, when all the fallen trees had been removed and roads and footpaths cleared, I received a surprise phone call one morning from my brother Paddy.

"You better get up here to the compound," he said.

The Old Bill had gone through the lorries like a dose of salt, recording every fault on the wagons. There were hundreds of irregularities. They produced a charge sheet about ten pages long.

So it was off in front of the beak I went. I pleaded that we were carrying out a public duty removing all these fallen trees for the public, and it was wrong for them to penalize me now.

My pleading did me no good. I think the fine was around £2500.

On top of the fine, there was also a problem getting paid by PJ McHale. But that's another story...

One of our first old Hymacs, 1988

7 | NO COMMITTEES, PLEASE

I have never been a great believer in committees or partnerships with people. I don't think there is anything wrong with them — it's just that I like to be my own skipper, make my own mistakes and choices. Committees just take too long to make a decision, and I rarely find that they all agree. I had to learn this the hard way.

I got a phone call one day from a friend of mine named Brian Cullen. He was a bricklayer. Brian was involved in a self-build group in Tarring, a small village near Worthing in Sussex.

"The committee asked me to talk to you to see if you will join our self-build group," he said.

I didn't know what a self-build group was, so Brian explained.

"There are thirteen of us, we are a mixture of bricklayers, carpenters, joiners, plasterers, sparkies, and tilers. Between us, we have all the skills to build our own houses, so we formed a group, got funding from a bank, found the land. We'll build our own houses. We run things as a committee, and we just need a groundworker to complete the team."

I didn't like the sound of the "committee." But I thought it over. I thought this would be twelve months of hard graft — every evening and every weekend for a year — but it meant I would have a £200,000 house with only a £50,000 mortgage. So I agreed to join.

Things went alright for a while. I did all the groundwork and drainage for the thirteen houses. The agreement was that we all did a certain number of hours as a group on each other's houses. Once we had completed those hours, we could then work on our own house.

As usual, I was very committed. I worked every spare hour. I brought some of my employees from the site to work on my house. Soon, my house was taking shape a lot quicker than the rest. I was putting in the hours, though, many times not leaving the site until the small hours. I still had my business to run, but I was full of energy and very driven.

It wasn't long before I started to hear a few comments from the other members.

"Why are you pushing so hard? Slow down, you're going too fast!"

The thing that they did not realize was that I was not going to live in my house like the rest of them. I was going to rent it out. When I explained this, they were a bit shocked, but I ploughed on, taking no notice of anyone. Every hour I could spare I was working on that house. Soon, it was completely finished.

It was a four-bedroom detached house. I laid white carpet throughout. But unbeknownst to me, the committee called a meeting behind my back. In that meeting, they decided that I couldn't rent out the house. Apparently there was some small print in the original agreement that stated that all the houses in the self-build must be completed before anyone could move in to a finished property.

No one told me this, they just let me carry on. What the committee did not know was that I had signed an agreement with a director of Shell Oil to rent out the property. Shell had their UK headquarters in Worthing, and she was moving to the area.

Now the shit hit the fan. All of this only came to light when she turned up with a removal lorry full of all her furniture. I had been telling these guys for weeks that I had rented it out. No one said anything to me. It was only when the lady turned up on site with a furniture lorry that they had the balls to ring me. In fact, it was the lady that phoned me, crying down the phone.

What could I say? I couldn't believe it. It would only get worse.

During the last few months of the self-build, there had been some sort of dispute between the committee and the bank that had lent us the money for the land and the materials. I can't remember all the details now, but the bank pulled out of our agreement. The self-build took the bank to court, and the bank installed security men on site.

Which house do you think they used as a security office? My new carpeted one.

Months later my Da rang me up.

"Go and have a look at that house down in Tarring," he said.

I hadn't been near the place. I couldn't bring myself to go near it after so much hard work, but I went and had a look. My house was covered in filth. Beer cans and KFC boxes everywhere. The security guys were just trashing it. I went mad and kicked off.

Next thing I knew, the police were there. When I explained the situation to them, they were sympathetic, but I still had to walk away.

To cut a long story short, I never did get the house in the end. I had to chalk it up to experience. I had been naïve and stupid. Another hard lesson learned. I swore never to get involved in another committee or rely on anyone else ever again.

The 4-Bed detached house I built in Tarring & had to walk away from, pictured 2020

8 | GETTING SERIOUS

The business was really starting to take off by the end of the 80s. Up until that point, I had been operating out of a small office under the stairs in my house. I was doing all the buying of materials, wages, invoicing, VAT, credit control, chasing progress on sites, and everything else myself. But it was just too much. I knew I would have to open an office and delegate if I wanted to grow the business.

Mark Schneidau, who had worked with me back with MJ Mansell a few years earlier, was doing the odd private tender and valuations for me. I asked Mark to come work with me full time. It was a big ask, as he had a family and mortgage commitments and was working with an established operator with a good package. But we sat down and talked. I knew it was a big move for Mark, but we made an agreement and put together a strategy for the business. Mark became our first full-time office employee.

Now I needed to find offices and a yard. Eventually, I rented a yard in Pease Pottage from a metal fabrication company. We installed two 40-foot sea containers and converted them into an office and a store. We were off.

A few years later, I bought a 20-acre site at Slaugham. We had our offices and yard there for a number of years before we bought our existing office site in Handcross High Street.

Our first office receptionist was Sharon Webster, the wife of one of our employees. She was very good. In them days, I was flying by the seat of my pants. Sharon was great at bookkeeping and keeping suppliers looking for payment at bay while Mark and I built up the business.

It wasn't long before we had around ten sites running for a variety of different clients. Our workforce was now around 40 men. One of the big issues in them days before electronic payments was going round all the sites on a Friday to pay the employees in cash. I used to do the wages on Thursday nights and go round the sites with a big bag of money on Friday. Many times, I had to meet the guys in the pub on a Friday night to pay them there. I carried an iron rod up my sleeve in case I was robbed. I was so happy years later when everyone was paid directly into the bank.

Now that Mark and Sharon were looking after the office, I was able to get round the sites a lot more. I had a foreman on every site, and at that time, almost all our employees were Irish. The Irish were synonymous with construction — and groundworks in particular — in the UK. The Irish were always great workers and fantastic characters. It's changed a lot these days, with Eastern Europeans now dominating construction in the UK.

Some of our office staff, very dedicated people

9 | DEADLY SITES

I have always loved getting my hands dirty and never missed a chance to put in a shift on site if need be.

One time, we picked up a contract at High Wycombe Hospital in Buckinghamshire, which was over 60 miles away from our base in Crawley, so I decided to rent a house in the town to save on the traveling. The idea was for the guys to stay in digs for the week and come home on a Saturday. The hospital was built on a hill, and our contract was to construct new accommodation blocks for the nurses. The new accommodation blocks were built further up the hill looking down on the hospital.

One day, I was on site operating an excavator loading lorries with my good friend, Dublin Chris. At 10 am, we stopped work to go to the café for breakfast. The excavator that Chris was operating was a temperamental old girl. The levers down the side of the operator's seat that allowed you to move forward or backward kept sticking. The machine was also a bugger to start in the morning, so once we got her started every morning, we filled her full of diesel and just let her run all day. That's how we left her, ticking over, as we went for breakfast.

When we came back 45 minutes later, we could only see one excavator at the top of the hill. Jesus Christ! We ran up the hill and saw the Liebherr embedded into the side of the hospital canteen. Our hearts were pounding as we ran down the hill. The whole arm and half of the machine were inside the canteen. Luckily, no one was hurt.

It was a miracle, thank God. We quickly brought the other excavator down the hill and attached chains around the embedded machine and proceeded to pull the machine out. The outside walls of the hospital collapsed around the machine. There was dust and glass everywhere. Some hospital management staff ran over to us to stop us, but we got the machine out.

I knew if these people had their way they would've made more of this than it was. Mind you, it was very bad. We got the machine out and back up the hill. Very soon, we had the Health and Safety Executive (HSE) on site, along with a BBC TV news team.

The site was shut down for a few days as the HSE pored over the machine to see why this accident had happened. But they couldn't find anything wrong with the machine, and we weren't going to mention the sticking levers. After a week's delay and a long report, they put it down to an act of God.

That was a lucky escape, but the next one was even luckier.

I couldn't believe my luck on this job. We had never had any real safety issues on any site. A few days after they allowed us to start work again, I was driving a site lorry loaded with stone. While driving slowly, down the hill I pressed the brakes. Nothing.

"Oh, Jesus!" I yelled.

I kept pumping and pumping the brakes, but still nothing. Everything seemed to go into slow motion. I drove the lorry up a grassed embankment, and she rolled over on herself into the staff car park. Miraculously, the lorry never hit any of the other cars. She was now sitting on her side.

I was standing up in the cab, looking out the window. The cab was starting to fill with smoke. The driver's side window never worked, so I couldn't wind down the window to get out. I started kicking at the windscreen.

As smoke filled the cab, I was afraid of the engine bursting into flames. Everything was happening very quickly, but also in slow motion. I know that doesn't make any sense, but that's how it seemed.

Luckily, some doctors heard the commotion and came running out of the hospital. I tried to shout to them to open the window of the passengers door, as this was my only escape. I'm not sure how, but they broke the window, and I scrambled out, exhausted and sweating.

I said my prayers. I will never be that lucky again. To cap it all off, Chris was at the other end of the site and never saw any of this.

When I walked around the corner towards him, he shouted, "Where's the wagon?" I just burst out laughing, though I could have started crying.

We brought Chris's excavator down and lifted the wagon back onto its eight wheels. The chassis was bent, but we dragged it back up onto the site and cleaned up the mess. A couple of hours later, you would never would've known it had ever happened. Now I just had to try and explain everything to the client!

We have been very lucky over the years with accidents on sites. Construction is a dangerous game. Put that together with incompetent people and it's a recipe for disaster. I have always believed in training internally within the company, especially regarding health and safety. We have a very competent advisor in Peter Hayles. But even with the best advice and good practice, accidents can happen.

In 1987, I had a contract to lay a main sewer directly under Crystal Palace's football ground for a new Sainsbury's that they were building next door. The job involved laying the sewer inside an underground tunnel. Usually, we would do this work by cutting an open trench in the road, but because of utility ducts and cables and a London bus route, we had to carry out the works through a tunnel. Before digging the tunnel, we had to dig a shaft down six meters to the correct depth to enable us to excavate the muck from the tunnel. We had never carried out this sort of work before, and most of our lads were frightened of excavating a tunnel.

It was left to a good friend named Mad Roy and myself to dig the tunnel.

We took it in turns, excavating the muck as we progressed works inside the tunnel. The air was getting thinner and it was very hot down there. The tunnel was five x three feet, so it was very small inside. Only one person could work at a time. I would work for three hours, then Roy would do three hrs. We only wore a pair of shorts and a pair of boots because of the heat down there.

After a week or so of excavating, we were about fifteen meters in. I was excavating away with the small CP9 jackhammer at about 11pm one night. There was no daylight down there, only artificial lights, so it didn't matter if it was day or night. Because we were alternating every three hours, we kept going 24 hours a day.

I was down there cutting away with the jackhammer, when I heard the strangest noise. I'd never heard anything like it before. I stopped work and looked at the ground around me. Everything looked alright. The wooden shuttering that we used for supports all looked fine, so I carried on.

Ten minutes later, I heard the same weird noise, so I stopped work again. This time, I could see the cracks in the tunnel walls slowly opening up around me. I dropped the jackhammer and turned to face the shaft. I tried to scramble towards the shaft.

"Whoosh!" Was all I remembered hearing. It happened so quickly. The tunnel collapsed around me.

I half made it into the shaft, which saved my life. There

was meant to be a lookout on duty all the time while Roy and I worked in the tunnel. Where was Rasher? He was our lookout guy. He was away having a smoke.

Mad Roy heard the tunnel collapse and climbed down the shaft to dig the muck and chalk off my back and legs. He got me out eventually. Finally, Rasher put his head over the shaft entrance looking down.

"What happened?" He asked.

"You'll know what happened when I get up out of this shaft!" I shouted at him.

Off he ran. We never saw him until about two weeks later in The Fox. Luckily, the anger had all gone away by then.

This is the sort of thing that can happen. Because of incidents like these, we are a very health and safety-conscious company. Over the years since then, we have won many awards for health and safety, and we continue to drive that message to all our employees.

10 | DODGY DEALING

Over the years in this business, you end up meeting and dealing with all sorts of crooks, chancers, conmen, and downright gobshites. Luckily, I have mostly managed to keep these shysters at arm's length.

One time, though, I didn't see it coming.

Mark and I talked our way into a contract with the Mersey Dock and Harbour Company. They owned vast tracts of land at Sheerness Docks. We were contracted to turn over twenty acres of reclaimed land into car parks on the River Medway. The car parks were for the thousands of new cars that were imported each year into the UK.

Our original contract started out small, but soon developed into multi-millions. We decided to open another office in the docks to cope with the demand, and I promoted Nick Tyler, our contracts manager at the time, to oversee the contract. Nick had started with the company a few years earlier as a labourer, but I could see the potential that he had. So we developed and groomed Nick over the years, and he turned out to be a very capable operator.

Our contract called for us to import hundreds of thousands of tons of stone into the reclaimed land and then to resurface these vast areas with tarmac. This process involved hundreds of lorry movements every week. We came up with the idea of bringing the stone from East London, up the River Medway into the site by barge. This idea would cut out hundreds of lorry movements and save us months on the contract.

At first, we could only unload one barge on each tide, but after we got the hang of it it was two barges each tide. This was saving us a fortune, but it wasn't going unnoticed.

We also found that we could go onto the beach beside where we unloaded the barges and remove all the beach/shingle and use the stone as fill. We could reduce the beach by one meter for its full length, saving us hundreds of thousands of tons of stone. We used to let the beach replenish itself over a period of a few months and then do it again. This was another great money earner for us, but apparently someone from a birdwatching group on the Medway got wind of it and we had to stop that wheeze.As the months passed, the contract was going very well and we were building a sizable team at the docks. We were making great money, but I was getting asked for backhanders from different people at the docks. This was nothing new to me. I had dealt with corrupt council officials and inspectors over the years. This was not my way of doing business, but sometimes you have to hold your nose and get the job done.

It could be port officials, union reps, or building inspectors. They all came out of the woodwork looking for a backhander. I had never seen a place like it.

We went along with this for a bit, but after a while

certain people were getting greedy. They were buying Mercedes cars, Harley-Davidson motorbikes, and showing off. It was getting ridiculous. We were all going to end up in the dock.

It got to the point where I bought a dictaphone and started recording every meeting I was in to try and protect ourselves. There was a lot going on, but I think it is better to let sleeping dogs lie. When new contracts came up to be renewed, we simply declined them. Greedy people make mistakes, and Mark and I decided to walk away from Sheerness and close the office. Those contracts and the easy money just weren't worth the risk anymore.

Besides, we had so many other opportunities presenting themselves.

Removing the beach at Sheerness

11 | MY FRIENDS FROM ABROAD

Never judge a book by its cover. Oh aye, I know. Here's one of the oldest clichés around, but it rings truer than an arrow.

Whenever you meet anyone, hold off on judgement. Don't assume anything, because you really don't know who they are and how they could possibly help you. Meeting two completely unassuming Kenyans back in 1991 pretty much changed my life. And Sinead, my second daughter, was born in June. What a year 1991 turned out to be!

You wouldn't know by looking at Sarki and Ali that they were multi-millionaires and owners of incredibly, wide-ranging business portfolios. Their money came mostly from owning the biggest brick quarry in Kenya, which they still have today. When we first met, they were doing a lot of property development in London and bought an old hotel site at Gatwick Airport.

It was an old, run-down place. Through a friend of mine, we got the contract to rebuild the place.

Mark dealt with them initially, and the deal was we'd get paid in cash every month. There was no contract. Everything was done on a handshake. They were bringing huge amounts of currency into the UK, and it wasn't uncommon to pick up £30,000 in plastic carrier bags.

Back then, I was in the office a lot of the time because

there was so much to work on. but I'd often turn up at this hotel site in my shirt and tie after 5pm and get cracking with one of the diggers. I still liked getting my hands dirty.

One night, I noticed there was an old boy walking around in a battered pair of dungarees, picking up nails which had been hammered off and knocking them back into shape for the carpenters to pick up the next day. All the other boys on the site were laughing at this old boy. Thing is, they had no idea who they were laughing at.

I was driving the digger from 5pm until 8pm most nights, and Sarki had called Mark to ask who this suited up guy that turned up each night was. This went on for weeks — me grafting and his odd nail mending — before we finally began chatting.

What a lovely bloke. So down to earth, no airs or graces at all. It took me a while to realize this was the top man of the whole operation. As weeks turned into months, Sarki told us one day that there had been a coup in Kenya, causing a government change. They would have to stop construction for a while until he could get more funds out.

I spoke to Mark, and between us we agreed that we would fund our works on the hotel until Sarki was able to bring more finance from Kenya. This really surprised them, but I had built up a bond with Sarki and Ali and really trusted them. They were dumbfounded, but really appreciated the gesture. It goes to show the strength of a handshake.

After a few months, with the new government embedded in Kenya, things went back to normal, and Sarki paid us the funds that we were owed. Just before the new hotel opened, I pulled Sarki to one side. I was trying my luck here, but if you don't ask you don't get.

"Sarki, can I borrow £500,000?" I asked him.

He gave me an old-fashioned look and asked what it was for. I explained that I wanted to move the business on. We were doing very well on the construction side of the business. We were making good money, but I was ambitious. I wanted to start a property development side to the business. I had formed another company and was putting things in place to take this forward.

Sarki thought for about 30 seconds, then said, "Are you still working on the new PC World showroom at Staples Corner?"

Of course I was. At that time, we were constructing the new flagship showroom for PC World, the biggest in the UK. I nodded.

"Okay," he said. "Meet me there tomorrow at 10am."

That night I hardly slept. What did he mean? He didn't say no, but why meet him there?

Next morning, I was up at Staples Corner bright and early, keeping my eyes open for the old boy. Sure enough, there he was getting off a red London double decker bus. Sarki didn't drive. I hadn't really thought about it, but I wasn't expecting him to get off a bus.

"Show me around the site," he said.

I showed him this massive cavern of a store. Halfway round — we were talking about nothing, really — he pulled out an envelope and gave me a cheque for £500k.

Wow. Half a million pounds! I couldn't believe it. We did a deal and shook on it, and that was it. No contract, no paperwork. Just a handshake. When does that ever happen these days? Proper old school.

I paid Sarki back the £500,000 and some interest within a year. I asked for £1 million. Again, no problem and again, all on a handshake. These deals with Sarki allowed me to bypass the banks with their rules and endless credit committees. I wasn't held back by red tape or any restrictions around my neck. It also meant I had the cash to back up my offers on any land that we were going after.

Many days, I went out looking at sites with Sarki. He would talk to me for hours, giving me the benefit of his vast knowledge. He lived in London. I would pick him up at a train station, and we would go off for the day. He always carried a Tupperware box with his lunch in it. He never trusted anyone to cook his food, only his wife. Many times, I tried to coax him to come into a pub for some lunch, but no way. It was against his religion to drink alcohol and he'd only eat his wife's food.

Sarki had a bit of a chip on his shoulder about English men. He never trusted them and thought everyone was discriminating against him because of his colour. I tried to reason with him many times, but there was no convincing him. He trusted me because I was Irish and not English and because I had put the money up when he couldn't get funds out of Kenya years before.

He asked me to front some planning applications for him. I was white, he reasoned. I would get it no problem. But sure enough, I got knocked back on the planning as well. Still, you couldn't convince him.

Sarki and I ended up doing many deals over the years. He could be a stubborn old bastard at times, but I learned many lessons from him, and I still deal with his family to this day. But none of them will ever lace his boots. He was one of a kind, and I have missed his company these last few years.

Keep 'Er Lit

Poser

12 | LIFE'S A BIG LEARNING CURVE

While getting the property development business off the ground, I had also been in talks with Russ Waddington from IGS about getting into the gas business. Russ operated a gas installation company based in Brighton. We met through some mutual friends. As I said before, I would never have any partners again, but Russ brought an opportunity for us to expand our business with me still keeping control of this new venture.

Russ had been in the utility business most of his life. He was very knowledgeable and had great contacts. Between us, we formed a company that could provide the house-building industry with a new concept.

We saw an opportunity to form a one-stop shop, providing clients with the installation of gas, electric, water, and BT ducting. These installations are usually done separately by individual entities. We would provide all the infrastructure and connections under one roof, so the client had only one point of call for all the utilities on his site. We tried it with a few housebuilders, but we were way before our time and it was slow to take off.

So Russ informed me one day that we should go for this new £20 million national gas connection contract. At this time, our small gas company only had about ten employees and half a dozen vehicles. I have always been a very optimistic and positive person, but how were we going to compete on a multi-million pound contract?

"Leave this one to me," Russ said.

There was a meeting called by the Gas Board for all the national contractors who were interested in this contract. We met at this big function room at a London hotel. All the big boys were there. The meeting was to explain the contract to everyone at the same time.

Russ and I walked into this big, packed room. I thought we were wasting our time there. I didn't think we had a chance. But as I watched Russ work the room, the patter just flowed from him. I couldn't believe the bullshit he was spouting, but it was all believable. He could have sold snow to Eskimos, that's for sure.

Over a period of a few weeks, the Gas Board whittled down the contractors. We were still in the running. They called us into a meeting with them to look at our strengths and weaknesses. We agreed that I would keep my mouth shut at the meeting. Russ would do all the talking.

And boy, could he talk. They whittled the competition down further, and we were still in it. They decided that it would be between us and two other contractors. They wanted to come to our office to see our setup.

"We're going to get this," Russ said. I was slowly starting to believe him.

On the day that the Gas Board came, Russ was just

flowing. I listened in amazement. It just goes to show you the old saying about smoke and glass.

At the end of the day, we came second for that contract, and rightfully so. We had no call being anywhere near that level of contract at that time. But I had learned that individuals can make a difference, and surrounding yourself with the right people is key to everything.

And as my old man used to say, "Don't believe all the bullshit you hear." In business, as in life, there are a lot of lessons to learn. I definitely made my fair share of mistakes, too. Some of these mistakes hurt financially. Some hurt your pride. In hindsight, family life also suffered, I thought I was managing everything alright, but the reality was that I didn't manage the family side of things the best I could have. And the family suffered because of that.

I know I can't turn the clock back, and that's a big regret.

* * *

As I headed into my forties, I was still working every hour of the day and looking for opportunities where I could find them. I had been dealing with a tarmac surfacing company from Portsmouth for a while. I got on well with the owner Phil O'Rourke and his wife, Theresa.

One day, Phil explained to me that they had been having some cash flow problems. He asked me if I was interested in taking on some contracts that the company had with

Kent and Surrey highway departments. Always with an eye for a deal, I said we would have a look at it. So one Saturday morning, Mark and I drove down to the south coast to meet Phil and Theresa.

After going through the company books at Phil's office, we all went to a local pub for something to eat and a few pints. We got on well with Phil and Theresa. They were down-to-earth people, and we ended up doing a deal with them.

When we left to go home late that afternoon, Mark and I were congratulating each other on a good day's work. We had agreed to take over Phil's company and all his contracts. What we didn't know was that this morning's work would end up costing us over £1 million in the long run.

Everything went well at the start. Phil and Theresa were two grafters. They lived and breathed the business. The work took them all over Hampshire, Surrey and Kent, and most contracts they undertook were profitable.

The problem was the council highway contracts. These just bled money away. We tried to get the company out of these contracts to no avail. I should have done more homework on the council contracts. That was a big mistake. Another lesson learned.

I also opened a builders' merchant with Phil in Havant called Fayejenn Trading. This was a big brand new unit, and it went well at the start. I should have realized that I had too many balls in the air. It took a while for the penny to drop.

I was travelling up and down the A24 to Portsmouth every day and getting home late every night. Although we had closed the Sheerness office, we still had the Handcross office and now the Havant office. It seemed like I was always playing catch up.

At Handcross, we now had around twenty staff in the office. Although we had very good people working for us, I was only starting to learn how to delegate. Nowadays, I am a great believer in delegation. What's the point of employing managers if you don't allow them to manage?

After a lot of sleepless nights, I realized that we would be better off shutting down the Portsmouth office. I have the scars on my back from that adventure. We have tried different enterprises over the years. But we'd come to the conclusion that it is better to stick to what you know. No more going off on a tangent. Another lesson learned!

* * *

I had been living in the Crawley area since we first came to England in 1973. But now I was looking to move out more into the countryside. I had earned a few quid by this time, and with the girls starting to grow up, I wanted something a bit more secure and quiet. So when I found Jamesland Farm in 2000, I couldn't believe my luck. It ticked all the right boxes.

The 11-acre property was a twenty minute drive from

Crawley. The village had a great family atmosphere. Although it was well out in the country, the school bus called right outside the door for the kids. Mind you, even then they still sometimes missed it.

Over the years, I had been making and saving a lot from the cash jobs that I had. When we bought the farm, my Da went to the solicitor's office with two Tesco carrier bags full of cash to make the payment. You just couldn't do that these days.

There was also a great little pub called the Bridge House in the centre of the village. Everything in them days seemed to happen around the pub. I met some great people in there, and big Fergal Tierney really sticks out. A proper man. If you wanted any news or gossip, you headed to the pub. Sometimes the landlady would even leave us in there on a Saturday afternoon and go shopping. We just left the money on the bar. No one would dream of taking advantage. Sometimes, it seemed like you were going back in time in that pub.

I bought the farm from Norman Handy, a guy I knew from years before in Crawley. Norman lived there with his family, but his wife Chrissy had been trapped in one of the horse boxes in the stables attached to the farm. She took an awful battering from a horse. So they decided to sell the property. They didn't move far. In fact, Norman moved back into the village a few years later. Sadly, Chrissy had died.

We were really happy living in the village and it was a

great place to bring up kids. Over the years, we extended the place and built a gym and swimming pool. Throughout the year, all the family used to come down and use the pool. We held many parties in that place.

One year, my sister Maria and her husband Harry got married there. We had a great big marque in the back field with hundreds of people there and a live Irish band playing. The next day, we used the marque again for a BBQ and a singsong with all our Irish relatives that had come over for the wedding. It was unbelievable.

I converted some of the old piggery into a storage yard that I used for the business. That didn't go down too well with the local council, but that's another story.

After a few years living there, I had taken up golf. We formed a little golf society down in the local pub. I had started a local development as well, where we found we had literally thousands of tons of topsoil to get rid of. So I came up with the idea of building a nine-hole golf course at the back of the property. I killed two birds with one stone!

I started moving the topsoil from the site to our new proposed golf course. Some of the nosy neighbours weren't having that, and I had a visit from the enforcement officer from the local council. To cut a long story short, there was nothing that the council could do, so a few months later, our local golf society had a new course to play on.

It was great! Sometimes I would come home from work, play nine holes, then have a swim. You couldn't beat it.

Sadly, a few years later, the local pub was forced to close, and the village was never the same after that. A lot of village life revolved around the pub. I suppose things moved on, and we all had to change.

Ross Waddington talked us into the last two on this £20m contract

Setting out on one of our earlier housing developments

13 | OH NO, NOT AGAIN

Everything on the business side was going great at the time, so occasionally I would go for a weekend drink with my mates down the pub. No big deal in that. Mostly all our socialising revolved around the company — either taking out clients and entertaining them or just going down the pub with some of the guys from the site.

One Friday afternoon, a lot of snow came down and we had to shut all the sites. So I ended up in the pub with one of our gangs. After closing time, we headed for a late night club to carry on drinking. I called a taxi about 2am to go home.

I had used this taxi company many times. They had a fixed rate for the trip from Crawley to Copsale, which was about fifteen miles. This particular night, when we arrived at my house, I got into a row with the taxi driver about the cost of the fare. The taxi driver wasn't wrong — I was. I suppose after twelve hours of drinking, I wasn't thinking right.

I made a bad choice and ended up punching the guy. He was totally innocent — just out doing his job, and I was right out of order.

The guy contacted the police and I was arrested. Although I had not been in any sort of trouble for twenty years, I did have a history of fighting, and when the Horsham magistrate looked at my past record, he gave me three months in prison.

I couldn't believe it. I thought for sure he'd give me a big fine or community service, but three months in prison was well over the top. I was stunned, but nothing was going to change. I was going to prison again.

I was taken from the court to Highdown Prison in Surrey. I went through those big gates in the back of a prison van, and all of a sudden, experiences from twenty years before were flashing through my mind.

I put myself into a different mindset. That's how you survive in prison. Lying in a cell that night on my own, I just couldn't believe how stupid I had been. The taxi driver was only doing his job. I was the asshole. I was running a successful business with a great family, everything was going great.

And now I was back in prison.

The next morning, I had to see the prison governor to decide if I was going to stay in Highdown or be moved to another prison. When the governor looked at my notes, he couldn't understand why they had sent me to prison. He saw that I was running a business, had a family, and hadn't been in trouble since my teenage days.

"Tell me what happened," he said. I explained, and he said that he was going to try and send me to Ford Open Prison.

"Normally, Ford wouldn't take any inmates that have been convicted of violence," he told me. "But after looking at your notes, I'm going to make a recommendation for you."

For the next two week or so, I waited to hear from the prison office whether I got the move to Ford or not. In Highdown, you were locked up in your cell 23hrs a day. On my first night in Highdown, I had a single cell. Later, I was moved into a cell with two other guys. This wasn't ideal, but beggars can't be choosers.

Thankfully, after two weeks, they were going to move me to Ford. As they drove me from Highdown to Ford, the route they took down the A23 almost passed in front of our offices. It was surreal. I could almost see our offices. I shook my head in disgust at myself as we passed them.

Ford had a totally different atmosphere. It was almost like a holiday camp. There were no cells. You shared a dormitory with around ten other guys. Although there weren't any locks on the door, after lights out there was no nonsense like I had seen at Blanytre House all those years before. The dormitories were clean and there was plenty of space, unlike Highdown. We were allowed to join various education classes during the day, and the food was good.

One day, I went and sat in the prison chapel. Although I had been brought up a Catholic, I had not been to Mass for more than twenty years apart from maybe a wedding or a funeral.

As I sat there thinking, the chaplain came in and we

started talking. He asked me some searching questions, and I had no answers. He got me thinking about my faith again. When you don't have many other distractions, it's easy to start seeing things more clearly. I started thinking maybe that old magistrate at Horsham had done me a favour.

Since that meeting with the chaplain, I have not missed a Sunday Mass. I've developed a more well-rounded view of life.

The time in Ford went by very quickly. Mark was looking after the business and had told clients that I was away on holiday. My sister Maria, who worked in our buyer's office at the time, was very helpful. In fact, everyone pulled together, and it gave me time to reflect how lucky I was with my family and the people around me.

Still, I promised myself that I'd never go back to prison again.

14 | INVESTOR IN PEOPLE

I have always believed that it's very important for any organization to develop its own people and promote them through the business. We very rarely used outside agency staff. Almost all of our managers and directors started out as site labourers within the business. We are always on the lookout for people with the right attitude. Once you have the attitude, you can develop it and teach new skills.

I never thought when I started out that I would be spending my day looking at cash flows, programming, accounts, and balance sheets. These were all things that I taught myself. I also insisted that all our managers could look at a set of business accounts and understand a balance sheet. They also needed to really understand how a business functioned beyond just the numbers.

I actively attended evening courses to learn new skills. I joined new groups like Sussex Enterprise, The Institute of Directors, The Gatwick Diamond, The Supper Club, British Chambers of Commerce — anywhere where I could pick up knowledge and learn from like-minded people.

At Sussex Enterprise, I was one of the founding members of the Construction Forum. This was a group of architects, surveyors, lawyers, accountants, and investors. I was the only contractor in this group. We met monthly to look at different issues within the construction industry affecting the Gatwick and Sussex area. Our company also ended up picking up contracts from the networking I did through the group.

I remember speaking to Mark about making a big financial investment in training. He was of a different mind to me at the start. He reasoned that we would invest heavily in our staff, and that they could leave at any time to go and work for Joe Bloggs down the road for an extra £5 a day.

I reckoned that if we invested in the staff, they would recognise and appreciate that. In fact, they were more likely to stay with a company that looked after and developed them rather than jump ship to a company that didn't care about them.

So we set out in 2000 to try and achieve an Investor In People (IIP) award. When I first contacted them, they were surprised. No construction company had ever earned the award at that point, I was told.

It was a two-year process. The IIP people went randomly to all our sites, talked to all our people, and got great feedback from them on what training they wanted and required. Our guys talked freely to these assessors. Some feedback we got was not very flattering, and that's fine. But mostly people appreciated working for the company and were very happy to undergo any extra training.

So we put in place a specific training plan for every single employee. We had to take on a new office manager just to coordinate between the assessors and our guys. It was really taking off. We were very open with everyone and held meetings out on site to get feedback from the site guys. What I didn't want was everyone to tell us everything was great and nod their heads. For this to work, everyone had to be honest, and we really encouraged people to speak out.

I'm sure there were people who were frightened to say anything detrimental at first. But soon, we were getting real conversations going. It was all very open. We really learned a lot.

It was not all plain sailing, and there were hurdles to get over, but we eventually got buy-in even from the most skeptical of workers. You can't give baloney to people — they see through it very quickly.

Another project we introduced was a quarterly company newsletter called *The Nugent News*. The idea initially was to let our guys out on site know what was going on within the group, what new contracts we had won, what new plant and machinery we were buying, and any staff gossip.

I thought, "Why just restrict this to employees? We should send this to suppliers and clients, tell them our story as well."

Soon, people were asking me when the next *Nugent News* was coming out. It was a great idea and a great way of letting everyone within the group know what was going on.

After two years of this process, we finally achieved the IIP award. It had cost a fortune, but we viewed this as an investment in the business. Over the years, we have invested millions of pounds in plant and machinery, but the biggest asset any company has is its employees

Over the years, Mark and I have been lucky enough to employ some very loyal, dedicated, and trustworthy people. We have a fair number of guys that have been with us for over 20 years. Most people that have come to work alongside us appreciate our attitude, and our staff turnover is very low.

I never believed in using outside agencies, and we have always promoted people internally. I have lost count of the number of people who started with us as labourers and ended up as directors of the company.

My sister Celine has overseen our office for many years. She looked after all the accounts, but she always had my back as well. She never took any nonsense from any of the men. I was lucky that after Celine left the business, my daughter Sinead took over the same role. She is thankfully following in Celine's footsteps.

It has been a privilege to have worked alongside the likes of Micky and Jason Crowe. Micky started with us over twenty years ago and brought his young fifteen-year-old son, Jason, onto the sites on a Saturday morning to put some manners on him. Jason now runs his own sites for us, very successfully.

I remember when Richard Webster started for the company as I mentioned before, he was just a sixteen-year-old way back in the early 1990s. He was working under his father Jackie Webster and learning the game the hard way, still all these years later Richard is a great example of attitude and work ethic, I think at one time we had about seven Websters on the company books.

Patsy Scullion is another old hand. When Patsy, Joe McDonnagh, and Tom Harvey came for a job back in 1996 at our site in Eastbourne, it was them that interviewed me, not the other way round!

Joe Dwyer and Andy Nye are another two guys that stand out. Without them and others like them, we would never have had the success we've had over the years.

At one point, I remember almost all our employees out on site would have been Irish. But since the rise of the Celtic Tiger in 1995, we have not seen as many young lads coming over from Ireland looking for work. There's plenty of work in Ireland, and young lads now just don't seem to want to get their hands dirty. Now the vast majority of employees we have are from the Eastern European countries. There's no more Murphy — more like Kowalski or Petrovic now. These guys all have a great work ethic and have become part of the family very quickly.

Guys like Milan Pavic, Bes Ramij, and Linas Girkantas have all adapted very well to life in the UK and all run very successful sites for us in various parts of England. I believe they are very much the future of the company.

I didn't want a trophy or a nice logo on our company

letterhead to advertise the fact we had achieved IIP status. What we wanted was to instill a sense of learning within the workforce, a will to do better. We wanted an organization where everyone was free and willing to speak out.

After we received accreditation, I never renewed it with the IIP. I didn't need to. We developed our own in-house training. With the help of our site employees, we developed a quality assurance procedure. Now every employee within the business has different levels of NVQ qualifications assessed by outside adjudicators.

Our aim was to be the John Lewis of construction, and I think our clients have recognized that over the years. Mostly all of our contracts are repeat business from the same clients. Training has paid off in so many ways.

Through all the networking I was doing, and the awards that the company was achieving, I was asked to do a few public speaking events for Sussex Enterprise and the Construction Forum. I am not a natural public speaker, but once I got onto the subject of training in the workforce, the words flowed very easily.

Along with some other business leaders, I was invited by our local MP Laura Moffatt to the House of Commons for lunch, and to look at how we could develop business within West Sussex, I couldn't believe it. A wee lad from Belfast sitting having his lunch in the House of Commons. A few years later, I had the same invite from another MP, Nicholas

Soames, who showed me around the whole Palace of Westminster and the House of Lords.

I knew I was making headway.

One of our training classes

Big difference from the old man's days on the sites

Always believed in practical training

15 | UNDER THE SPOTLIGHT

Now that our business was really growing, I knew we would have to find new premises. We owned our existing premises on twenty acres of prime Sussex countryside, but the local planning authority would not let us expand the offices in an Area Of Outstanding Natural Beauty (AONB).

Luckily, we found a site in Handcross High Street. It had belonged to Richard Branson, and he had operated a small airline company there before he started Virgin Airways. When we first moved in, there were a lot of air stewardess uniforms still in the cupboards.

"This is your new uniform," I joked with the office girls. But they wouldn't have any of that!

We had around twenty office staff. A friend, Martin Andrews, who was a celebrity agent, suggested that he could get Chris Eubank, who was a world champion boxer and celebrity at the time, to cut the ribbon.

"Hmm," I thought. I could invite the press and perhaps generate a bit of publicity for the company. I told Martin to go ahead. We agreed to terms, and Martin started inviting the press to the opening.

At about 7pm on the night before the opening, Martin rang me. I could tell from his voice there was a problem.

"Eubank wants another two thousand pound or he's not

coming," he said.

I thought Martin was joking, but he wasn't. Eubank also wanted extra money for his driver.

"Give me his number, Martin," I demanded, but Martin declined. "You can tell Eubank to fuck off!" I shouted down the phone. "I will go to the press now with this! We had an agreement, and now a matter of hours before he was due to attend, Eubank is asking for more money. It's wrong, Martin, just wrong!"

I'll ring Brian Quinn. He's the Lord Mayor of Crawley and a good friend. I'll see if he can step in, but I'm going to the press with this tomorrow."

At about 11pm I received a call from Barry McGuigan.

"Listen, Len," he said. "I know what's happened. Do you mind if I do the appearance and cut the ribbon tomorrow? If I do it, you can't go to the press."

"Ok, Barry," I said. "I'll see you in the morning."

Unbeknownst to me, Martin had called Barry. Knowing that I was a big fan of Barry's, he'd asked him to cover for Eubank. The next day went off without a hitch, and I took Barry around to some sites that I owned to get publicity shots of him cutting the first turf. I would use these for years.

Barry McGuigan was great that day. He really went out of his way — talked to all the staff, even to passing strangers watching all the commotion. An absolute gentleman.

A year or two later, I was staying in the Europa Hotel in

Belfast. I had come to Belfast to watch Amir Khan and Laszlo Komjathi fight at the King's Hall. Barry was commentating on the fight for TV.

As I walked into the hotel restaurant to get my breakfast on fight morning, Barry called me over. He was sitting having breakfast with TV pundit Jim Rosenthal. I sat with them, and it was great to hear all the background gossip surrounding the fight. They invited me to the after-fight party that night in the Europa. I'm usually not into celebrities, but it was good to see a lot of the old boxing faces.

Another old face that I met one day was the botanist David Bellamy. I was at the Tower of London one afternoon to pick up an award on behalf of the company. We had been put up for the Green Apple Environmental Awards by the British Chambers of Commerce.

Prior to the awards, we were in the Great Hall having lunch. I was seated next to this guy who I sort of recognized, but only very vaguely. He asked me what we had done that was so environmentally great. I told him we had done nothing. What I had done was come up with a way of reusing concrete and steel rebar. I was getting two uses out of things that would have been sent to the landfill.

"To be honest, I never gave the environment a second thought," I told him. "I was trying to save money, not save the world."

He gave me an old-fashioned look.

After lunch, they announced that David Bellamy was going to introduce the winners. The light shined on this guy I was talking to minutes earlier.

You would never have known it was him the whole time I was talking to him. But as soon as the light shone on him, he was into character. His show business persona was all a front.

I was called up to receive an award from him. He put the microphone in front of me.

"What great thing did you do to receive this award?" He asked. I could have kicked him, but I blagged my way through an answer and gave him a sly wink when I finished.

It was a real surprise and great honour to be named "Irishman of the Year" in 2005 by the Celtic and Irish Cultural Society. Ever since my Da brought the family to the UK in 1973, we have never forgotten our Irish roots and have always been involved in different Irish groups, clubs, and societies.

It was also a real privilege that other people had recognized the works that we had been doing. My Ma and Da had always taught us to give someone a hand, not a boot, and I have always carried that philosophy with me.

Although we may be living in places other than Ireland, being Irish is always with us. In all likelihood, only Irish people will understand that statement. I believe that it was being Irish that gave me both a healthy disrespect for the establishment and a "can-do" attitude. Irish immigrants in many countries have always faced racism and discrimination, I think that's where we get that famous "Fighting Irish" attitude from.

I, for one, am glad to have it.

Growing up in Belfast is the one big advantage that I think I have in life. I never took any educational exams when I was younger, or went to any university, or earned any degrees. Fair play to anyone who has been to university and has gotten the degrees, but I was lucky to be born with that Belfast streetwise gift. It has helped me see the opportunities in life and take advantage of them. You just can't teach that in a classroom.

In 2007, we started a project for Mansour Namaki. We constructed the groundworks, basement and concrete frame for Palladio, off Bishop's Ave, Highgate. It was sold for £35 million in 2008 to Lev Leviev, an Israeli diamond billionaire. At the time, this was the most expensive property in the UK. *The Sun* did a big feature about it on its front page.

We had constructed several projects for Mansour, but this was by far the biggest he — and we — had undertaken at this point. Mansour was a Iranian who had come to the UK in his teenage years and made his money selling ink cartridges for photocopying machines. Somehow, he fell into high-level developments.

When I first met Mansour, there was a fair bit of haggling to be done over our price for the job. Phil Read, our surveyor for this project, handled most of the haggling on our end. The house was on probably the most expensive street in London. Ringo Starr, Lulu, and Maurice Gibb were all neighbors.

Mansour would come to the site every day to chase progress. He would argue over the cost of a bag of cement. That was just his way. He was a very demanding client, but he really knew what he wanted and how to get it.

Because of the site's tight boundaries and the fact that the building took up nearly the whole footprint of the site, we had to figure out how to actually build this massive development. I had driven up to Manchester to buy a crane, which I reckoned would just about fit onto the site. We brought the crane down to London on four low-loaders. It took about three days to erect the crane, and the celebrity neighbours were not too impressed with all the noise and activity. The crane did the job and ultimately paid for itself on this one project.

My brother Paddy was the foreman on the job. As usual, he really pushed the men and the project. One day, Mansour rang me up.

"Paddy is pushing this too much," he said.

I couldn't believe it. Mansour was always pushing me, and I was always pushing Paddy. Now we were being told that we were going too quickly!

Next time I saw Mansour, I asked him about the speed of the project and why he had suddenly changed his mind. It turned out that there was some holdup with bank payments to fund the project. That was the real reason why we were being asked to slow down.

This taught me a good lesson about how outside matters could have an impact on how projects are funded. I was a lot more aware after that.

Eventually, the project was finished. It was amazing to see the finished project. Mansour had spent £500,000 on the garden and landscaping, £1.5 million on an ornamental stone staircase, and £100,000 on a bulletproof front door.

The list goes on. What a property...

Near the end of this project, I had gotten to know Mansour fairly well, or so I thought. I asked him for a meeting one day.

"Come to the office," he told me.

I put the hammer on him for a £1m loan/investment for a starter home development that I was looking at, but had not sorted the funds for yet. I thought Mansour would be a passive investor, and I agreed to give him a 10% return on his investment. He laughed at me and took me into his side office and showed me a slab of marble.

"This marble can only be found in one part of the desert in Iran," he said. "It costs £5,000 per square meter."

That's what excites me, not starter homes. I never got the investment, but it's taking the opportunities when you see them is what matters.

There are a lot of wealthy individuals out there. Never be embarrassed to ask them to invest!

Barry Mc Guigan presenting me the IIP award

16 | THE FINANCIAL CRISIS

In January 2006, I brought Doug Chivers into the business to run our property development business Jamesland Homes Ltd. Right from the start, I knew that Doug would be a great asset to the group. His energy and enthusiasm just flowed, and he proved to be a great managing director of this business. We started to see results very quickly.

Doug had made some good contacts at Heritable, a private bank based in Berkeley Square in the city. Over the next few years, we used the Heritable Bank a lot, as well as Close Bros and Sarki for the expansion and financing of Jamesland Homes. Very quickly, we had sites in Goudhurst, Angmering, and Tunbridge Wells. These were all good quality sites in middle class areas. We tried to keep away from building starter homes and concentrated on homes starting at around £500,000.

We were also lucky to catch a growing market. Very quickly, this business was turning over in excess of £5 million a year. All told with all our businesses, we were turning over £20 million plus a year. We were still hungry for new sites.

One particular site that Doug had been nurturing for a while was an old hotel in Hawkhurst owned by a husband and wife team. Doug really liked this site and had done a lot of work with the owners to buy the site, but they kept messing him around at the last moment. In the end, they told us they were going to put the site in an auction and we could bid for it there if we still wanted it.

Doug had offered them £640,000 which we thought was more than fair, but they thought they could get more at auction. So on the morning of the auction, Doug, Naomi (our sales girl), and I were on the way to the auction in Maidstone. We received a call from the Heritable Bank telling us that they could no longer support our bid for the hotel, as their legal team had found a problem with the title.

Doug was gutted, as he had put a lot of effort into this site.

"Forget the bank," I told him. "We'll find the money somewhere else. I don't know where, but we'll get it."

To cut a long story short, we ended up buying the hotel for £570,000 at the auction — £70,000 cheaper than we had offered the owners prior to the auction. Stupidly, they had not put a reserve on the site and were now obliged to sell it to us.

We were over the moon. we had gotten the site, and at £70,000 less than we had previously offered. As we went to register our solicitor details with the auctioneer, we were approached by some people from a production company working for the BBC. They had filmed the auction, for a new television series that was going to be called "Under the Hammer."They asked if they could follow the story of the build. We agreed, and the whole process was filmed over a twelve-month period and shown primetime on the BBC.

During the next twelve months, we also acquired sites in Borden, Felbridge, and Horsmonden, among others. We were all very ambitious and had this great "can-do" attitude, and people were starting to recognize this. We were getting offers of land from all sorts of places and a lot of very interesting opportunities.

Within that next eighteen-month period, we grew this business to over £10 million a year. But we were still hungry. We were then approached with an opportunity to take over another regional developer in Kent called Pentland Homes. After doing extensive due diligence on the company and after numerous meetings with the Heritable Bank and the sellers, we offered them £11 million for the business including their large land bank.

It was the land bank that we really wanted. Along with Doug and our management team, we put together a business plan that would grow the business to £50 million over the next five years. The Pentland Homes deal took us nearer that target. In February of that year, we had also been recognised by *The Financial Times* as one of the top 100 growing construction companies throughout the UK.

During the early months of 2008, we started to hear the early rumbling of financial problems within the market. We took a great interest in this, but never dreamed it would end like it did. The first signs that we started to see were when some clients started taking a lot longer to pay us. We went through our usual credit control procedures to retrieve payments due to us, but suddenly clients that we had dealt with for many years started going into liquidation and owing us a lot of money.

Some of these clients were national companies. Ballast Wiltshire was the first to go, owing us £50,000. Over the next few months they were followed by Greenacre (owing us £300,000), Quintenglen (owing us £70,000), Pierce (owing us £150,000), Oakvale Homes (owing us £75,000), and Jarvis (owing us £75,000).

It was like a never-ending bad dream. Now, instead of growing and pushing our business, we were fighting to keep it alive. Towards the middle of the year, one of our bigger clients — Oakdene Homes — went into liquidation, owing us over £300,000. That was a big hit in many ways, as they had been funded by Heritable Bank, the same bank we used for Jamesland Homes.

We had clients going bust on us who owed us a total of £1.6 million. It was all hands to the pumps in the office. It was obvious to us that this whole financial mess was not going to end well. During this time, the office lights would still be burning long after 10 pm most nights as we tried to save the business.

We decided to set up another company that was clear of any debts, and Mark was tasked with getting the new company up and running while I dealt with existing suppliers and clients. It seemed like I was going to a liquidation meeting every other week for one of our clients that had gone bust.

Everything was very negative at this time, and I knew this was taking its toll on me, although I tried to hide it. All the newspapers, TV stations, and media were full of this negative news. Northern Rock Bank was the first of the major high street banks that showed signs that it was in trouble, but it wasn't the only bank. It was quickly followed by NatWest, Royal Bank of Scotland, and Barclays.

What the hell was going on? we had never seen anything like this. We had come through many recessions before. But nothing like this.

In early October, Heritable Bank went into liquidation. The shit really hit the fan. At that time, Jamesland Homes owed the bank £9 million.

We had assets of over £11m in that side of the business. We had done nothing wrong. It was the bank that went into liquidation, not us. It was the bank that broke their contract and commitments to us. But it was us who had to pick up the pieces.

At that time, we had a lot of negotiations with the insolvency practitioners appointed to run the bank during liquidation. We agreed to buy our £9m debt back from them at a reduced price. Doug and I went to the city and other institutions to raise the funds. We also looked at other options open to us to pay the bank off. We thought we had done a deal with Close Brothers Bank in the city. They had agreed to lend us the £9m in principle.

Two days after getting this offer from Close Brothers, Lehman Brothers Bank went bust. All deals were off. The world markets crashed, and along with them any chance we had of raising the finance we needed.

In the background of all this, I had also been working with Sarki to privately raise the funds. I did a deal with Sarki, and he could give me £6 million in liquid cash. That was all that he could get his hands on. We thought the insolvency guys would go for that, but no. They now wanted the full £9 million.

Another friend of mine, Michael Lord Castle, was also working in the background for us trying to raise the funds. In the end, it was almost impossible to find anyone to lend the funds unless it was against an exorbitant interest rate. The whole financial world was upside down.

So we sat down with the insolvency guys again and ended up doing a deal with them. The bank would release the funds to us to finish the sites that we had, bearing in mind that the total sales for these sites we were predicting was £11 million. The deal was that the bank would get their initial £9 million back, and anything over that amount would come back to us.

Given the circumstances, it was the best we could hope for. We knew we had good sites and were confident of attaining the predicted £11m sales. That meant we could walk away from the whole mess with our £2m profit.

Doug did a fantastic job over the next eighteen months and finished all our sites on time and to budget. We also attained the sales prices we were predicting. We sold the lot for £11 million, which was a remarkable feat in the market of that time. We knew from the start that we had good sites, and we were confident of attaining those sales figures.

The problem was that the insolvency practitioners from the bank reckoned that their costs from administering the bank during this period were £2 million. We would be getting nothing.

What a big lesson this was! They were a bunch of lying, conniving, stealing bastards, and there was nothing we could do about it. These guys were meant to be professionals, but I had met better people back in Pentonville nick twenty years earlier.

At the end of the day, when all the dust had settled, we had to put Jamesland Homes into liquidation ourselves. The bank had literally legally robbed us. All we could do was learn the lesson.

As all this was going on with the Heritable Bank and Jamesland Homes, our groundworks business was also fighting to survive after losing £1.6 million from clients going bust on us. It was almost inevitable that we would have to close that business. We had previously experienced over 25 years of continuous success and growth with almost no bad debts, but the recession and financial crash of 2008 were too powerful. It was a massive lesson for us all.

Very quickly, we restructured the whole business. Gone was our property development company Jamesland Homes. We closed Nugent Groundworks and other associated companies, and in 2010 we formed Lenmark Construction Ltd. This was going to be a joint venture between Mark Schneidau and me. We both had a 50% share in this business. Early on, we decided that there would be no bank borrowing anymore, no overdraft, nothing from a bank.

We still had the scars from our earlier experience. And that decision to avoid banks would serve us well over the years.

I eventually moved to Malta but was still very much involved in the business for a few years. It was Mark that took on the challenge of the new business. He has quickly grown that business to turn over in excess of £10 million per year. We will always be in control of the business. We will never let a bank dictate any terms to us in future.

Mark has now been joined in the management team by my daughter Sinead — who has been the company accountant for many years — and Barrie Rossiter, who started with the company many years ago as a site labourer and has progressed through the business to be our construction director.

Between the three of them, the business is in very good hands. Barrie and Sinead have recently put together a business plan that will take us through to 2025, although the 2020 pandemic may change things!

Much of what I have learned over these last 35 years in business is not to put all your eggs in one basket. Especially in terms of clients.

Also, to grow a business, you must learn how to delegate. Don't be afraid to delegate. Don't be afraid to take chances, but beware of industries/businesses that you know little about.

Invest in training your staff — they are your best asset. I have always surrounded myself with smarter people than myself. It's so important to have trust in the people around you, especially your management team.

Lastly, beware of consultants. I have found that these people are mostly chancers, just salespeople with a fancy title trying to put their hand in your pocket.

Keep 'Er Lit

Mark Schneidau & Doug Chivers taking a day off in Malta

Barrie Rossiter & Mark Schneidau, I am lucky to have these guys running the business, along with Sinead

17 | THE ISLAND IN THE SUN

I knew the business was in good hands, so moving to Malta in early 2009 was a no-brainer for me. After dealing with the negativity from the sharks and hypocrites at the banks for the last twelve months, I needed to rest my brain and do some soul-searching.

I had a property in Malta that I bought years before, so accommodation was no problem. I asked Zoe to come to Malta with me, but she wanted to stay in Sussex to look after her mother. I couldn't blame her for that. But over time that distance between us dampened the flames, and unfortunately over time we drifted apart, and that dampening became irrevocable.

Zoe is a great lady and a great mother, but I had just fallen out of love. It happens.

As soon as I arrived in Malta, I joined a night class at The Malta College of Arts, Science, and Technology to learn Maltese. I continued night classes for three years. The first exam I ever took in my life was in Maltese. The language is a mixture of Arabic, French, Italian and a bit of English. A real mixture and a real challenge, but I thought that if I was going to live in the country, I should at least try and learn the language and culture.

Luckily, I had already made a lot of friends on the island.

I joined a local boxing gym to keep my fitness up. Eventually, I arranged to bring my old amateur club from Crawley over to the island to fight a Maltese select team. The event was a great success and was also televised on Maltese television. The sponsorship from my old friend Michael Lord Castle really helped. It was such a success that the Crawley club then invited the Malta squad to the UK for a rematch later in the year. Great friendships have blossomed from there.

After being in Malta for around a month, I had to return to the UK on business. I received a phone call from my friend, Spiro Brincat, back in Malta.

"The police have towed your car away," He said.

"Don't worry, Spiro," I told him. "I'll sort it on my return."

When I got back to the island, I went to the police station and was told that I hadn't paid any registration tax on the UK vehicle, they were impounding it. They wanted £42,000! in tax.

I explained that the vehicle was UK registered and that I had paid VAT in the UK and wasn't required to pay tax in another European country. Also, I had already paid £46,000 for the car. Why was I going to pay another £42,000 in tax?

I eventually talked them into giving me the car back, but the same thing happened about a month later. The car ended up in the police pound, and I couldn't get it back.

I went to a local solicitor and explained my problem. He was no real help, so I went to the embassy and they were no real help either. They told me some things are a bit quirky in Malta. I argued with them, but got nowhere. They called security because I was kicking off. I just couldn't believe that no one was listening.

Eventually a guy came out of another office in the embassy and he told me that I was correct. He said that the Maltese government would not listen to his argument that they should not take registration tax from people from other European countries if the tax had already been paid in that country.

Finally, someone was listening to me. He put me in touch with a EU agency called Solvit. They were looking for a test case to take the Maltese government to court. They accepted my case right away.

After months of nothing happening, though, I told Solvit to forget my case. They were just a talking shop. It was going nowhere, so I engaged another solicitor and took the Maltese transport agency to court myself. It took almost another year to finally get to court.

On the morning of the court case, I had been warned by friends that my solicitor wouldn't turn up. Sure enough, they were right. Corruption in Malta is rife at every level. I couldn't believe it. After waiting all this time, they were now going to adjourn the case.

I pleaded with the court usher to let me speak to the court. I had been taking Maltese lessons for two years now and thought I could blag my way through. The usher came back to me and told me they would agree to listen to me without a solicitor and in English.

When I went into the courtroom, I was expecting a bench of three judges. Instead, I found a board of around twelve people. I spoke up for myself and explained my case. They asked me to wait outside, then called me back in. They agreed with me and told me to go and pick up the car from the police pound. I was given Maltese registration plates of TFI 002, which meant I had a tax-free registration and nothing to pay.

There was a nationalist government led by Lawrence Gonzi in place at the time. We were in the middle of an election. The Labour candidate Joseph Muscat promised the Maltese people that if he got into power, he would give the people back the money from the registration tax scheme that the Nationalist government had taken from them. Muscat was elected and eventually paid back millions to the people that had been conned by the Nationalist government.

My reason for going into depth regarding my case is to show that you should never give up. Everyone was telling me I had no chance. I was never going to win against a corrupt agency, but I stuck with it. I wrote hundreds of emails and letters. Eventually, I knew I would win. It would just take time and patience.

As the old man would say, "Don't let the bastards grind you down."

After living in Malta for six years, I took a call from Jim Nugent, a family member in Belfast.

"Is it ok if I come over to visit in a few weeks?" He asked.

"No problem, Jim," I told him.

"Do you mind if I bring a friend?"

"Sure, no problem. We have plenty of room."

A few weeks later, Jim arrived with his friend Mary. "Wow," I thought when I first met Mary. We hit it off right away. Mary was from West Belfast, just a few miles from where I was brought up. We were the same age and had the same outlook on life. We hit it off right away.

I was sorry when they had to leave at the end of the week, so I asked Mary for her phone number. Luckily, she gave it to me, and we kept in touch for the following months.

We had a lot in common. She liked the same things as me. We spent hours on the phone. Eventually, I asked her to come over to Malta for a week's holiday. We got on really well, and I met her again in Belfast a few weeks later when I was over there to run in a marathon. I asked Mary to come and move over to Malta with me, and after some arm-twisting she agreed.

Since that first day she moved in, we have never been apart. It's unbelievable, really. We are so alike and love doing the same things together. It was just meant to happen.

One of the great things that I love about Malta is the people. Sure, the weather is great and there is always plenty to do. There's a great social scene there. But the greatest asset that Malta has is its people. I have been blessed with a very close group of friends.

I first met Spiro probably twenty years ago when I first came to the island on a week's holiday. We loved the place so much that first week there that I bought a small flat just beside Spiro's bar in Birzebbuga.

I couldn't believe it. We only went for a week's holiday and now owned a flat there. The idea was that we would use it 3-4 times a year for family holidays.

Over the years, I have met all of Spiro's family. In fact, they have taken me under their wing as one of their own. I have been invited to family gatherings, BBQs, weddings, and funerals for years now. It feels like I'm really part of another family.

Every Saturday night in Spiro's bar, I would meet a group of guys. We would sit and have dinner and a few beers together. We have done this for many years now. Every Saturday evening until Spiro sold the bar around 2016. Now, the gang — Charlie, Sammy, Inman, Andrew, George, Spiro, Mary, and I — travels out to a different restaurant or village feast around Malta every Saturday evening.

We all get along great. There is always loads of storytelling and jokes, and the craic is great. In all these years, we have never had a cross word between us.

Sometimes, the gang would come over to our house for a BBQ or to watch a big game on the TV. Sometimes we'd go to Inman's house for a meal, or to Spiro's field for a BBQ. It's great to have genuine friends, and I was very lucky to find them.

Most years now, I organize a summer holiday for us all. Sometimes, it's a week in Sicily. We've also gone to Spain, Poland, Czech Republic, and the UK. Another time, we all went on a cruise around the Mediterranean.

I also organized a trip to Old Trafford to watch United vs. Tottenham. We followed that up with a flight over to Belfast for a few days, and then we went down to Dublin for St. Paddy's Day. They loved Ireland just like us. Great times with genuine people.

I bought some other properties in Malta and really grew to love the place, sometimes the corruption that you find there gets you down, but overall it was a great move to settle there.

Keep 'Er Lit

The Birzebuggia Feast, I havent missed our village feast in 18 years

Love this picture, Me & Mary out in Valletta

Leonard Nugent

The Maltese gang, with my Ma & Da, our weekly Saturday night dinner

Charlie, George, Inman, Andrew, & Spiro, genuine friends on holiday in Slovenia

Our Maltese gang up in Spiro's field having a late dinner

18 | 12 MARATHONS, 12 MONTHS, 12 COUNTRIES

At the start of 2011, I made a New Years Resolution not to drink any alcohol for the whole year. That was no easy feat in a place like Malta, where there is a very lively social scene. I had made so many friends there, and there were always invites to BBQs and parties.

I went the full twelve months. I never had a drink and actually enjoyed it in the end. It also gave me a different perspective on things. I was looking for a reason to keep it going. I was going to the gym every day. I was also out running most days and really enjoyed the fitness.

So around December 2011, I decided that next year I would do something that kept me occupied and focused. I came up with the idea of running a marathon every month. I had done a half marathon during 2011, but doing a full marathon was a different matter. And to do one every month was crazy. But I liked the challenge, and I thought I'd make it even harder by running each one in a different country. This would be a real achievement if I could pull it off.

I had never run seriously before, and I wasn't sure if I could complete the challenge, but decided to make it happen anyway. Trying to organize training plus work would also prove to be a problem. Not knowing where to start, I checked out various websites to find out where the

European marathons were held. I tried to plan ahead as much as possible.

During that year, I ran in many different countries: Germany, Israel, Spain, Ireland, Hungary, Austria, Italy, Malta, and the UK.

Getting to the right level of fitness for the first marathon was my first task. I would leave my house in Birzebbugia each morning for a five-mile run. Over the weeks, I increased my mileage everyday until I was running around 70 miles a week, with a long 20-mile run on Sundays. The heat in Malta was also a real problem, but over time I used this to my advantage.

I think everyone has a fear of the unknown at the start of their first marathon. But I was confident that I would see the finish line.

In addition to the twelve marathons, I also ran six half marathons and a few 10k races. My times for the marathons ranged from three hours, 50 minutes to almost five hours. After a while, I didn't really concentrate on my times. Just reaching the finishing line was good enough for me.

Most marathons are held at weekends, so I soon got into the habit of my monthly visit to the departure hall at Malta Airport. I would usually travel on a Friday, go to the expo of the marathon on Saturday, and run on the Sunday. I would try to see some of the city/country on Monday and fly home Tuesday. This became a way of life, with training fitting in around my work.

I found my toughest marathon in Jerusalem. This was for a number of reasons, the least being the torrential rain that weekend, plus the never-ending hills and climbs. This was my longest run at five hours, and I was ready for a good soak in the bath at the end. Jerusalem was also the best organised of all the runs. The organizers had done a fantastic job for the runners, but could not control the weather.

The security around the city was unbelievable. Growing up in Belfast, I thought I had seen it all, but Jerusalem was on a different level. There is also so much to see in the holy place. I stayed a week and still only saw half of the place.

The Dublin and Belfast marathons were very much alike, in that it never stopped raining during both of them. It started to seem to me that I would never run in the sun again! I think I was becoming too soft. After living in Malta for five years, I missed the Mediterranean sun.

In both Irish capitals, large crowds came out to cheer the runners on. This also really helped in the last few miles, when my wet clothes were sticking to my body and my legs were starting to feel heavy, although both courses are reasonably flat and fast to run.

Another memorable run was Fussen in Germany. This was a mostly off-road marathon through forests and lakes in the German Alps. With the Germans, you expected good organization, and our hosts did not disappoint. Of course, it rained again. I was starting to get used to it now.

Back in Malta, we lined up in Mdina for the start of the Malta Marathon. It started with a minute of silence for John Walsh. I had only recently started communicating with John through email after reading his column on a Saturday morning in *The Malta Times*. He was very helpful and knowledgeable and wrote some great little gems. The minute of silence was well-respected.

We seemed to be running around Ta' Qali for hours that day before joining up with the half marathoners at the halfway point. I was glad to see the ferries come in as we approached the finish line at Sliema. At least it didn't rain!

Around the middle of April, because of work commitments, I entered the Gozo Half Marathon. I decided to run it twice, giving me the marathon distance without having to travel abroad.

Starting was no problem, but as I approached the finish line in Xaghra, it was a bit deflating to have to start again. I picked up my medal, had a drink, and started to run the course again. It was a strange feeling running the course again on my own after being surrounded by all the other athletes during the first 13.1 miles. At around the eighteen-mile point, I took off my number, as I felt that people thought I was the last competitor. I was thankful for the bottle of water that I had hidden on the first run, knowing that the water stations would be all gone on the second.

After running four or five marathons in as many months, I found that my body was starting to adapt and I could cut back on training. I found that I could do a few five-mile runs a week plus a fifteen mile run on Sunday and my fitness level would be ok for the next marathon.

The one big thing that I learned during this period is the impact that having a good diet has on your body. I also became very knowledgeable about nutrition. I took an evening course on nutrition at The Malta College of Arts, Science, and Technology. I don't think I could have completed so many runs without carefully following a strict diet. I also did not drink any alcohol for the full twelve months.

Next on my list was Budapest. I had never been to Hungary before. The course was very flat and featured long stretches along the River Danube. The scenery was fantastic along the river, but I was more than happy to see the finish line.

Around mid-October, I realized that I was losing time to complete the twelve marathons in twelve months. I started to look at other options. I had learned a lot about my body by this point, so I decided to create my own marathon.

I decided to run from the tip of Gozo to the bottom of Malta. I actually started in Xlendi Bay and started to run to Mgarr. I stopped my stopwatch at the ferry and started again when I landed at Cirkewwa. The run to the south of the island was very tough. I bought some water at shops on the way, but really struggled on this run. It had actually turned into a 30-mile run by the time I stopped in the dark in Birzebbuga.

Another memorable marathon was the Malta Challenge Marathon in November. This was the first time I had competed in this three-day event. It was very different from all the other marathons that I had run. On Sunday, getting called to the front of the pack by race director Barry Whitmore was a shock. It was my birthday, and everyone clapped and sang "Happy Birthday!"

Running these marathons really helped me develop my willpower and determination. I soon realized that the real marathon did not start until around the eighteen-mile mark. This was when the body's natural store of carbohydrates would be depleted, and where your diet was so important. It was also where your mind could play tricks on you if you let it. I soon taught myself little ways of tricking my mind to get me through to the 26-mile point.

When I finished the last of the twelve marathons in December, I was unsure of what challenge to give myself for the next year. I found my inspiration in a book about Barefoot Ted and the Tarahumara. These were Mexican barefoot runners who lived on a diet of mostly beans, nuts and corn. They regularly ran huge distances of over 100 miles at a time.

After reading this book and doing some research, I gave myself the target of running a marathon barefoot. I trained early in 2013 and got up to nine-mile barefoot runs, but the Maltese roads are not the best even with a good pair of trainers. I used to go up to Ta'Qali in the north of Malta and train there in a park. But as spring turned to summer, the boats and boat life seemed to take up all of my time.

So I never ran a marathon barefoot. Maybe now that I'm living in Florida with great facilities all around, that could happen sometime in the future.

Belfast marathon

Just finished Austrian marathon

19 | THE CAMINO

"Can we do the Camino?" Mary asked me one day while we were out walking.

I thought she wanted to dance. She explained that it was a pilgrimage that had been around for nearly 1,000 years. It stretched from Saint-Jean-Pied-de-Port in France across the Pyrenees and along the length of Spain to Santiago de Compostela, a distance of almost 900 km.

This sounded like a good challenge. Although we are both practicing Catholics, our reason for doing it had nothing to do with religion. We wanted the physical challenge.

After doing a lot of homework on the internet, it was decided. Off we went to buy two airline tickets, two rucksacks, and some walking gear.

We thought we were ready. Our plan was to walk an average of 30 km per day and allow for some rest days in between. The whole thing would probably take around five weeks or so. We each packed a rucksack. Mary's weighed 12 kg, and mine weighed 14.

On January 12, 2017, we caught a flight from Malta to Paris. When we landed, we made our way across France to a small town on the French side of the Pyrenees called Saint-Jean-Pied-de-Port.

The next morning, it was freezing. But we were up and out of the digs just after first light, raring to go.

We had no idea what was ahead of us.

Pied-de-Port is a small town at the base of the Pyrenees. It was a 25 kilometer walk to our first overnight stop at Roncesvalles. We gained 1,400 meters of elevation in a day. About three km outside of Pied-de-Port, we started to hit snow. As we climbed, the snow got deeper and deeper.

By midday, we had probably only gone about 10 km. We were getting tired, and we still had to walk another 10 km to reach the top. The snow was getting stronger, with the wind cutting right through you. We put on our ponchos over our coats to try and keep the cold out, but it was hard just to walk. The rucksacks weighed heavier on our backs, and now the snow was around 18 inches deep. Instead of walking forward as normal, we had to lift each foot 18 inches in the air to take a step.

I swear this was the longest day of my life. I kept looking back at Mary. because I knew I was struggling. She may have been struggling, but she never moaned. She just sucked it up and ploughed on.

I was getting worried about losing the light, as it was around 3 pm and we still had around six km to go. The snow was so deep. We tried to eat some sandwiches we had bought earlier before leaving the village, but it was so cold that you could hardly take the gloves off your hands.

Some people had walked this path earlier in the day, and

we tried to follow in their footsteps to make it easier getting through the snow. But the stuff was coming out of the heavens so quickly that the tracks were filling up with fresh snow.

As we climbed higher, the snow got deeper. We were both knackered.

"What are we doing here?" I heard myself ask.

It was dark when we reached the summit, and we still had another kilometer to go to reach the monastery where we were sleeping for the night. The wind and the noise up there was unbelievable.

As we descended into the monastery just past the peak, it got quieter. It was like a Christmas card scene. When we arrived, we registered with the reception and were surprised to see so many people about. It was also here that we had to get our credentials stamped. This was a sort of passport that allowed you to stay at the Albergues on the way.

We later learned that almost all of these people started their walk from this summit, not the bottom.

Unlike the two eegits from Belfast.

We were given two bunk beds in a large dormitory with around twenty people. We didn't care. We just wanted to get a shower and something to eat and get into a sleeping bag. This was our first experience of the Camino, and very quickly we started to understand what it was all about. In the dormitory, there was no privacy. There was lukewarm water in the showers, and it was not the cleanest of places, but everyone was in the same boat.

There was a late Mass that night in the monastery. Mary and I went, and the priest gave us a blessing and wished us good luck with the walk. He knew we were going to need it. So we headed back to the dormitory and fell into our sleeping bags and the land of nod.

That would turn out to be the worst day on the Camino. I now understand why a lot of people give up after the first day climbing that mountain. It was traumatic and physically gut-wrenching. It was not for the faint hearted.

The next morning, we were up at first light. Our clothes were still wet from the previous day's snow, but there was no choice. After a quick breakfast, we headed out into the snow. We tried to walk in the road as much as possible, as during the night, they had snow ploughs trying to keep the road clear.

We both knew this would be another long day, but after about 15 km of walking, we began to descend from the mountain and started leaving the snow behind us. This made the walking a lot easier, and we soon got into a good stride.

Our plan was to try and do this walk on a budget of €30 per day between us. This included everything — food, drink, and lodging. We would be living almost like the pilgrims that had gone before us for centuries. But they never had the €30 that we had.

We stopped each night mostly in what are called Albergues. These are mostly dormitories owned by the local village or council where pilgrims can stay for one night only for around €5 per person. For the fee you would usually get a bunk bed — usually in a shared dormitory — a shared kitchen, showers, and a common room. You had to get your credential stamped at each albergue to prove that you had walked the whole way.

We soon got ourselves into a routine. We would leave the albergue at around 8 am, then walk for a few hours until we came across a local bakery or café and had breakfast. We would then walk again until around midday and try and find somewhere or something to eat, usually what the Spanish called a *desayuno*. Then we would walk through the afternoon until we had done around our 30 km target.

Some days, it wasn't easy to find an Albergue, and you would be walking round a deserted Spanish village in the dark looking for somewhere to sleep. Thankfully, this didn't happen too often.

When we did reach an Albergue, we would try and find two bunks near each other. Then we would wash our socks, pants, and vests in a sink. If you were lucky, there would be a washroom. We had three sets of underclothes each so that every day, at least we would have clean clothes to start the day. Because there wasn't always heat in the Albergues, the clothes would often still be wet. I'd hang my clothes off the back of my rucksack to dry in the morning sun as we walked.

After the first week of walking, we both had blisters on blisters. We knew this could be a problem before we started and had brought along plasters to make it easier, but it was still a daily problem. Mary used to tell me to "suck it up."

Each day, we were burning about 4,000 calories. The problem was that you couldn't find enough decent places along the route to eat and replenish the lost calories. I remember always being hungry. Soon, the weight was dropping off us both.

We both also realized that we had brought too much clothing with us, and so every other day we would throw something out of our rucksacks to lighten the load. If a piece of clothing didn't have two uses, out it went. This helped bring the rucksacks down to a more manageable weight.

When we eventually did finish the walk, we had the strap marks of the rucksacks embedded into our backs. These took a long time to go away. Sometimes, when we were out walking without the rucksacks months later, it felt like we were still carrying them. They had become a sort of phantom limb.

We met some great people along the way. They came from all over the world to do the Camino. I had never heard of the Camino before Mary mentioned it, but this walk was widely known throughout the world. We met a lot of Korean people doing the walk, and they told us about this famous Korean author who had done it and wrote a bestseller about her experiences. So they wanted to experience it. We met people from Canada, Europe, the USA, Africa, and everywhere you could think of. The world was represented on the Camino.

As the weeks passed, we seemed to get stronger and were walking at a good pace. Getting proper food was still a big problem, but we were starting to enjoy it.

Also, some of the characters we met along the way really made us smile. They made the journey a bit easier. There were three young Spanish kids at the albergue in Hontanas, a small deserted town in the middle of nowhere. These lads were only about seventeen or eighteen years old. They had almost no money and a dog they took everywhere.

We met in the middle of winter, and there was no heat in the place, and only cold water. We were all starving, and the albergue had no food, so it was a very long night. No one could sleep because of the cold and the hunger. We had no Spanish, they had no English. But between us we had a good laugh, and it was great to see young people who had no smartphones or tablets, no money, and were just so happy and free.

Days later, we came across them again in a village called Carrión de Los Condes. We had found a convent who let us stay for the night. I went outside at about 8pm to get some food and found the three Spanish kids sleeping outside the convent in some cardboard boxes. Apparently the nun, a mother superior, wouldn't let them stay inside because of the dog. And they didn't want the dog to have to stay outside in the rain by himself.

Anyway, I went and bought a load of food and a few bottles of wine. The €30 budget went out the window that day. When I came back, I found a back entrance and let the boys and the dog into the convent. We all went upstairs to the dormitory and we had a bit of a party. We couldn't speak a work of Spanish, and they couldn't speak a word of English, but a great time was had by all.

We must've made a bit of a racket, because the old nun superior burst through the door. She wasn't happy. She tried to kick the young kids back out into the rain. I wasn't having that and told her so. I don't think she understood the English words I spoke, but she got the message and relented, so they all stayed. The next morning, we were all up early and back on the road. It was another week before we met the Spanish kids again.

Most people who do the Camino usually take a week or two holiday and do a stage or two of the walk. They would usually take a few years to complete the full walk, but there were a few like Mary and myself that January who were doing the full 900 km in one go. We walked through many different regions of northern Spain. Through the Basque Country, into La Rioja — the red wine region — then onto Castilla y León, and — finally — Galicia.

While walking through a country, you really get a feel for the people and for the country. This was the real Spain, not like the tourist traps we all know on the Costas. The Basque people we found to be particularly friendly, while Galicia on the Atlantic Coast was very much like Ireland — very green, very wet, and there is a big celtic tradition and community there.

The Meseta Central plateaus were another part of Spain that we didn't know existed. The Meseta Central is not unlike a desert. In the winter, as we walked through it, we prayed for no rain, as there was just nowhere to shelter — almost no trees, just a massive, flat plateau of land. At night, it was freezing there. I'm sure in the summer it was the opposite, with nowhere to hide from the su., We were happy when we reached the end of the Meseta Central on the outskirts of Astorga.

When we reached a big city like Astorga, or Burgos, or even León, we used to gorge ourselves, because out on the trail you just couldn't find any home cooking, or even a fast food outlet. We knew we had to eat around 3,000 calories a day just to be able to complete the 30 km walk. But this was mostly impossible. We always looked for an Albergue that had a kitchen. Then we would go and find what vegetables and meat we could locally, and I would make a stew. I always made enough for any other pilgrims that were staying in the Albergue, and it always went down well with everyone. It was a flashback to the stew I used to make for the boys at 2 Spencer's Road in Crawley.

While most days we walked on average around 30 km, one particular day really sticks out for us both. We left the

Albergue in Hornillos del Camino at first light. We had some fruit in Mary's rucksack.

We found ourselves on an old Roman road. The Romans built their roads dead straight, and this day somehow we got lost. We ended up walking a total of 47 km to the next big village of Frómista. During the day, I had a feeling that something was wrong, as we never saw any people about. But I had a map, and I was reasonably good at directions. Any time we did get lost, I always headed towards the sun, as the sun sets in the west, and it west was the only direction we were going.

This Roman road went on for mile after mile, and it was starting to get heartbreaking. There was nothing around us — just the wilderness. We did see a train in the distance, and we thought about following the train tracks until we found some sort of human life. But we gave up on that idea and ploughed on, miles and more miles.

We only had an apple between us now. Mary would take a bite, and then I took a bite. The water bottles we had were now dry, and still we marched on. I thought about the Roman soldiers who had built this road, and how many of them must have died in the process.

The sun had gone down, and we were losing light very quickly, when I saw some sort of light in the distance. So we headed towards them. After another few miles, we came to the edge of a village and actually crossed the train tracks we had seen earlier.

It was also raining now, with only a few street lights letting us know where to go. We looked around the centre of the village for an Albergue, but couldn't find anything. I told Mary that I'd find a police station — at least we could rest in there.

So I started knocking on some doors to either find the police station or an Albergue. Eventually, someone answered a door and told us in broken English that he thought there was an Albergue that was open just up the road. We knocked on some more doors without any luck. I can imagine what we must have looked like to whoever opened the door, because we were shattered and covered in mud.

Eventually, we knocked on a door. It was a private house that took in pilgrims. It was like winning the lottery. There were four pilgrims already in the house. Once they heard that we had walked from Hornillos, they couldn't believe it.

They showed us where we could have a shower and they made us a meal. I don't know what the food was to this day. We didn't care. Food had become nothing more than fuel, and we needed it right then. We both cleaned our plates twice.

The lady who owned the house was called Lourdes, and her husband was José. Lourdes took Mary into another room and helped her bandage her feet. They were swollen, blistered, and bloody. She told us there was a hospital nearby, and we should go there first thing in the morning.

Eventually, we clambered into a clean single bed each. It was heaven. In seconds, we were asleep.

The rule in all the Albergues is that you can only stay for one night, unless it's a real medical emergency. Lourdes told us we could stay for a second night, as there was no way Mary could walk the next day. The next morning, we headed over to the hospital, and they cleaned up Mary's feet as best they could and gave her some medication for the pain. They told her to rest. Afterwards, we went back to the house to rest up.

Upon reflection, it was a toss-up between this 47 km walk and the first day climbing up the mountain for the worst day on the Camino.

Later in the afternoon Lourdes told us that she had taken a phone call from some local Spanish pilgrims who were staying that night, and that they had a dog with them. Our eyes lit up. It had to be the kids we had met earlier at Condes and Hontanas. We told her we thought we knew these lads. So I went out to the local shops and bought a load of veg and meat and cooked a big Irish stew for when they arrived.

It was great to see them again, and we had a great bit of craic with the three of them that night. After dinner, Mary started the washing up. There was some stew leftover. She went to throw it in the bin, but one of the Spanish lads stopped her.

"I'll eat that for breakfast," he said.

We both looked at him.

"I don't know when I will eat this good again," he said.

The next morning, sure enough, there was yer man eating the stew for breakfast. We all had to leave that morning. We all said our goodbyes. Unfortunately, we never saw those kids again which was a real pity. We told Lourdes that she might see us again in the future. I'm sure she's heard that before, but I was already planning something else.

Frómista is the halfway point of the Camino, and it was surprising how quickly Mary and I bounced back to health. I think my Irish stew played a part. We both carried on, mile after mile.

"Another few weeks and we would be in Santiago," we told ourselves.

After a few days back on the trail, we came to another mountain range. And just our luck, it had started snowing. So as we climbed the peak towards Foncebadón, our destination, out came the ponchos again. Sure enough, we walked straight into a blizzard.

We had seen some round stone structures in the fields that must have been used by shepherds in the winter. We thought about stopping there for a while, but it was just so cold on the mountain that we didn't want to stop for fear of freezing to death.

Just before dusk, we found the Albergue at the top of the peak. It was packed with pilgrims. Apparently, this weather up here was like this for weeks on end, and you could be stuck up here for a while. The food wasn't great in this place, but at least it was hot. Someone got a guitar out from somewhere, so there was a bit of a singsong with people from all sorts of nations. We had no problem sleeping that night, although the dormitory was absolutely packed with over 30 people.

The next morning, most people decided to stay indoors, as there was still a blizzard outside.

"Let's take a chance and walk to the next Albergue," I said to Mary. She agreed, and as we were putting on our ponchos and rucksacks, people told us we were mad to go out into that.

But hey, that's us! Off we went into the blizzard.

After a mile or so, I thought that we had made a mistake. But it was too late to turn back. So we ploughed on. After a few hours of slow walking, the ground levelled out and the snow started to thin out. We started to descend the other side of the mountain. Below us in the valleys, it was all green fields. We could just about make out the village of Molinaseca. It was like a different world that we were coming out from.

It started to feel like we had broken the back of this walk now. We only had about 250 km to walk, and it couldn't come quick enough. Day after day, we marched on. There were no more blisters. Our feet had become hardened to walking. But we still encountered the odd wild dog that would attack. This happened a few times, and you always needed to be aware of your surroundings. And of course we were always hungry.

We noticed that things started to change on the walk once we reached the town of Sarria in Galicia. There were a lot more people from this point on. Sarria is around 100 km from Santiago. If you walk from here to the finish, they give you a certificate to say you have walked the Camino. So a lot of people start in Sarria to get the certificate, although it is almost at the end.

A week or so later, as we approached the outskirts of Santiago, we knew we would finish the walk that day. I thought I would feel a sense of achievement once we reached the cathedral in the centre of the city, which was the finishing point.

But to be honest, both Mary and I felt a bit deflated. We had gone through a lot the previous 5-6 weeks and learned a lot about ourselves. Now it was over. What next?

We had been told by some pilgrims that in the old days, pilgrims sometimes carried on walking to Finisterre, another 100 km away right on the Atlantic Coast. This was the place in the olden days that they called the end of the earth. As Christopher Columbus had still not sailed to the Americas, people thought Finisterre was the end of a flat earth.

So we put the rucksacks back on and walked the 100 km to the end of the earth. When we reached the lighthouse at

Finisterre, it did feel like an achievement. We had done it! Looking out at the blue skies with the Atlantic roaring below us, we took out an Irish Tricolour that we had brought with us and let it fly. We both felt really proud and over the moon that we had made it safely.

Job done. We headed back home to Malta.

We learned on the Camino that we could really travel light. Many times, we would be going off for a weekend somewhere and couldn't get all our stuff into a small suitcase. Now, we realized that we didn't really need to take all this stuff with you. You only need what you need.

We had slept in some weird and wonderful places on the Camino, all on a €5/€10 per night budget. Whether it was an albergue, YMCA, school hall, or convent — even a mental hospital one night — whatever. We had learned we wouldn't be too fussy in future, and appreciated how lucky we actually were.

We finished our Camino at the end of February 2017. During that summer, while having a beer in a Maltese pub, I mentioned to Mary that in the old days, the pilgrims had to walk back all the way home from where they had started from on the Camino. We had taken a train then a flight to get home to Malta. What we should have done was walk it back from Santiago back across northern Spain and the Pyrenees to Pied-de-Port in France where we had started from, just like the old pilgrims.

"Are you mad?" Was all I heard coming back at me.

So we had another few beers. By the end of the night, we had decided to walk the Camino again, this time from Lisbon in Portugal to Santingo in Spain. Then, we would do the original route of the Camino, but this time backwards to Pied-de-Port in France.

I suggested that we then walk from Saint-Jean-Pied-de-Port up the Atlantic Coast of the Bay of Biscay to Bordeaux. This would be a walk of around 1700 km in total. Based on 30 km a day, I thought that if we started in October, we could make it to Bordeaux just before Christmas.

We shouldn't have gone for a beer that day!.

So on the 18th of October, we boarded a flight from Malta to Lisbon. I couldn't believe we were doing it again, but it was too late. This time, our rucksacks were only 8 kg and 10 kg. We had learned our lesson the first time. We carried only what we really needed, although we were going to be away for around three months.

That first night in Lisbon, we booked into a YMCA dormitory. The next morning at first light, we set off north towards Santiago and Spain. That late summer of 2017, there was a heat wave in Portugal. The temperature was around 27-30 degrees Celsius, so it was great to walk in shorts and a vest, and we were well used to the rucksack.

We followed the same routine as the previous Camino, aiming for around 30 km a day. It was a lot easier to get proper food along the Portuguese route. This made a big difference, but the near 30-degree heat every day did take its toll on us. We fell into our sleeping bags every night exhausted.

We walked towards Fatima, the famous Portuguese shrine where Our Lady had appeared in 1917, then northwards along the coast towards the city of Porto. We rested here for a few days and did some sightseeing. We really needed the rest, as the sun was unforgiving every day. But our bodies had gotten used to the 30 km trek every day. We never really suffered from blisters on this walk, and the scenery in Portugal was so different from the Meseta Central in Spain.

As we walked and talked each day, a lot of the time we were in our own little world. Nobody knew who we were or what we were doing. We also had time to think and use our minds as we hiked mile after mile up the coast. We had gotten into a routine of talking, listening to podcasts, talking, thinking, and talking. It was only when we stopped for some food that we got the chance to talk to anyone else.

After leaving Porto, we called at the villages of Vila do Conde, Marinhas, Viana Do Castelo, Carreço, and Caminha. In Caminha, we took a ferry across the River Minho into Spain. We were sorry to leave Portugal, as we both really liked the people and the country.

Now, we made our way through the Spanish countryside towards Baiona. We knew Baiona well, as we had been here the year before with our catamaran. It's a great little port, with a lot of history. This was the spot that Christopher

Columbus landed after sailing back from America.

After Baiona, it was another hike up the coast to the city of Vigo. We had a rest day in Vigo to do some sightseeing. We really liked the old town, especially where the fishermen lived in Casco Vello.

The next day, we were up and out of the YMCA where we had stayed and headed for Pontevedra. Most of the walking to Pontevedra was on main roads. The majority of all the walking that we had done was on hiking trails through the countryside, and it was on these country trails that you met real people, the people who work the fields. We found that the majority did not speak any English. But it was never really a problem if we got lost or needed something. We always found a way to communicate with people.

Pontevedra itself was a lovely old historic town, all cobblestones everywhere and small little streets. We found the Albergue and got our heads down. Tomorrow was a 25 km walk to Calas De Reis. Another three days of walking after that and we would be in Santiago again.

There wasn't much to see in Calas de Reis, so we headed on and eventually arrived in Padrón. it wasn't a big town, but it had a lovely town square in front of the cathedral. We had no problem in getting an Albergue here. The next day was another 25 km day. We left the albergue the next morning at 5am to get to the pilgrims' Mass at midday in Santiago.

The route was mostly along main roads and some

bypasses. You really needed to be aware on these roads. Sometimes you were only 6 inches away from these 40-foot artic wagons, and it seemed sometimes that the wind from the wagons would suck you in below the wheels. We were always happier walking through the fields and countryside.

We made it in good time for the midday mass, and it seemed really strange to be back in Santiago again. There was a sign welcoming visitors to the city, and we stopped and had a few photos taken there.

From Lisbon to Santiago, we had walked a total of 640 km. Our bodies had gotten used to the walking — that was no problem now — but the heat that late October made it a lot harder. We spent a few days in Santiago just to rest up. On the 12th of November, we started the 800 km walk back to Saint-Jean-Pied-de-Port in France.

When you walk any of the routes to Santiago, there are arrows that give you the direction to go. I assume that these have been put there by the different pilgrim societies, or just helpful farmers and locals. Sometimes, you won't see these arrows for a few miles at a time, so you really need to be aware and alert. Now, we were walking against the arrows back towards France. It became a whole lot trickier to keep on the right track.

We also got told many times by pilgrims, "You're walking the wrong way." When we explained that we had already walked the route and we had decided to walk the other way, they mostly started in disbelief.

We experienced a lot of rain in that first week walking towards France. It was always a problem getting our clothes dry when we reached the albergue, as a lot of these places were only used in the summer and didn't have any heat for the winter. Also, a lot of the albergues were shut, only opening in the spring, summer, and early autumn months. Many times, we got to a village only to find the albergue shut. We would have to walk on to the next village. Sometimes, that next village could be another 10-15 km away. This could be heartbreaking.

As the days rolled by, we kept to our 30 km target as much as we could. It was on my birthday on the 27th of November. That day, we reached Frómista, the halfway point of the walk to France and the home of Lourdes and José, who had sheltered us during our first walk in January. We were in bad shape when we first arrived at their door in January after walking 47 km with only an apple to eat all day.

Now, we were a lot fitter and better prepared. When we explained to them that we had completed the first walk and had carried on to Finnisterre, then started a few months later from Lisbon to Santiago and would now carry on to Bordeaux, they couldn't believe it.

It's unbelievable what hardships the human body can put up with and adapt to, if only people can make their minds as strong as their bodies. But that's a different story.

The next morning, we were on the road before first light.

We wanted to reach Pamplona in the Basque region to meet our Spanish friend Fernández on the 1st of December. It helps now looking back at the photos and a diary that Mary kept to remember dates and places. A lot of the time, roads, villages, fields, and albergues all just all morphed into one.

As we climbed the peaks leading to Pamplona on the 1st of December, it had started to snow again. When we reached the city centre, the snow was now about 4 inches deep across the ground. Walking with the rucksacks became a whole lot more difficult.

We had a great meal that night in Pamplona with Fernández, then left early the next morning. But the snow was a lot deeper. We had heard rumours during the day that our route over the Pyrenees had been closed because of snow. We needed to try and find another route while keeping to the original path as much as possible.

We eventually ended up walking towards a place called Zubiri. We arrived there late that night. The snow was around 8 inches deep, and we had kept to the roads as much as possible, as they were so much easier to walk on. The official path was through fields and countryside, but it was impossible to walk on these with all that snow.

Arriving late that night, we couldn't find anywhere open to buy some food. This had been a continuous problem — getting enough fuel into our bodies to enable us to walk the distances that we needed to walk. In the morning, we were up and out of the Albergue fairly early looking for a bakery or something similar to get some breakfast.

Back in Malta, we would have porridge every day for breakfast, and this would keep us going until lunchtime. Here in the mountains of northern Spain, you ate what you could get.

Luckily, that day was only a 20 km walk. At the end of the day, we would be back in Roncesvalles at the monastery, where we had ended our horrendous first day on the Camino nearly twelve months before.

There was no more snow falling now, and it was great to walk along these almost deserted roads covered in snow. Every corner and turn we took was like a Christmas scene from a Disney movie, and we were in a really happy mood as we approached the monastery.

After booking in with the Peregrinos — these are the guys that run the Albergues — we headed up to the dormitory for a shower and change of clothes then down for a great big feed. The next morning, we would be walking down the mountain, leaving Spain and heading into France.

Our last day on the Camino.

That night, we met a group of six guys around the fire who were just starting their Camino. They were full of questions for us both, desperately looking for tips and advice. We were exactly the same eleven months earlier.

It's a big thing to walk across a country. You just don't know what you are in for. We had experienced a lot, learned so much, and gained a lot more appreciation of our surroundings. Although we were both practicing Catholics, we hadn't done the Camino for religious reasons. We'd done it more for the physical challenge.

Still, I know this experience made our faith stronger and our outlook better. As we left the monastery the next morning and started to descend the mountain. I couldn't help but flash back to eleven months earlier. Literally, the blood, sweat. and tears climbing that bugger of a mountain. Now, as we descended it, I'm sure there was a grin on our faces. Halfway down the mountain, the snow started to melt away. Soon, all we could see in the valleys below us was luscious green fields and pastures full of sheep and cows.

It was like a different world as we reached Saint-Jean-Pied-de-Port late in the afternoon. All around the main Camino office there were fresh-faced pilgrims all waiting to get their Camino passport signed before they started the long trek to Santiago. When we reached the office and I asked the Peregrino to sign our passports for the last time, he looked up at us.

"Wow," he said. "There's not too many people that walk it back."

We smiled at him and told him we were now walking to Bordeaux to catch a flight back to Malta.

He smiled and shook his head. "Now I've seen it all," he said.

Before we headed out and found an albergue for the night, we had a few beers and planned the route we would take for the 250 km walk to Bordeaux. We decided to try and make this walk as easy as possible. I found a route that would take us to Biarritz on the Atlantic Coast. We would then walk up the A63 through the national park called Les Landes, a massive forest of 10,000 square kilometers of pine trees that expands out to the outskirts of Bordeaux.

The A63 runs right through the forest, and that seemed to be our easiest route. But we found that even in December, this route was just too dangerous for us to walk on. We had many close encounters with speeding trucks and cars. So we decided we would head into the woods and follow the numerous trails that crisscrossed the forest, making our way slowly north.

The big downside to this idea was that thousands of years ago, the entire forest was under an ocean. Nowadays, the whole forest was built on sand. The sand was actually worse than snow. It just dragged at your calves. It slowed us down a lot.

At this stage, we were probably making just 20 km a day. But even at that pace, we would still make it in time before Christmas. Most days, the sun was out, and it was glorious walking through the forest. We will never forget the smell of the pines. Sometimes, we didn't see people for days. There were different small hamlets within the forest where we would stock up on fruit and water to eat during the day.

Finding somewhere to eat at night was still a problem. We tried to find local bed-and-breakfasts to stay in.

Sometimes, we could find a youth hostel. On the odd occasion that we couldn't find somewhere to sleep, we had to splash out on a small hotel.

Walking through Portugal and Spain, it was mostly easy to stay within our €30 per day budget. But here in France, that was impossible. It was just so expensive. The differences in eating habits between the countries were also obvious. If you go to any tourist resort in Portugal, Spain, or France, you are going to find all the usual fast food places. But when you start walking off the mainstream, you really do start to notice the different foods and cultures of these different countries and regions.

Eventually, we started to come out of the forest. First, we noticed the industrial factories and lights. We hadn't seen these for a long time, and we didn't miss them. Now, as we walked towards the city centre of Bordeaux, it became very urban and busy. We found a small hotel near the main railway station and booked in for a few days.

It was the 15th of December. All the shops had Christmas decorations and toys.

It just seemed so different from where we had just walked from. We went to a Christmas market in the city centre and enjoyed the whole Christmas atmosphere about the place. After a day or two, we booked a flight back to Malta.

"We've walked the whole way from Lisbon to here," I said to Mary. "1Lt's forget the taxi to the airport and walk it."

"No problem," she said.

So the next morning, the rucksacks were back on for the 15 km walk to the airport. In some ways, it felt really strange to be walking to an airport. But in other ways, it felt so natural.

What a year this had been! In early January, we didn't know what to expect. We didn't know what the Camino was. Now, a few days before Christmas, it was all over. We had walked a total of 2600 km in that eleven months with just two rucksacks and ourselves for company. We had met so many different and unusual people along the way. We'd had so many great experiences, just too many to mention here.

Every night we walked the Camino, Mary would put a post up on her Facebook page about that day's walking and adventures. We used to get loads of comments, and we really appreciated those, especially from Christie Ballie and Corp Kelly in Belfast. They never missed a day making a comment, and it really lifted our spirits. In fact, it was very humbling getting comments from all our friends. It was the one thing that we looked forward to at the end of a hard day's slog.

We would recommend this experience to anybody. Who knows what the future holds? We could end up doing it all over again.

2nd day of our first Camino walk

Leonard Nugent

Took this shot when the sun was just right

up in the mountains

Leonard Nugent

Crossing the Pyrenes mountains

Crossing the Messetta plains in Northern Spain

Most days we sat at the side of the road for lunch

Keep 'Er Lit

This is the route we walked on the 2nd Camino from Lisbon to Bordeaux

The lighthouse at Finistere, the end of our 1st Camino, we had been saving the tricolour

Just arrived in Santiago after 800+ kilometres

The snow got deep as we crossed over the Pyrenees mountains

Leonard Nugent

Walking up the bay of Biscay shore towards Bordeaux

Coming down the french side of the Pyrenees, fantastic views

20 | LIFE ON THE OCEAN WAVE

Living so close to the sea in Malta, it would have been crazy not to get into sailing. That said, I waited quite a long time before really taking the plunge and learning the ropes properly.

One day in Vittoriosa, Mark and I went to the Valletta Boat Show just to pass some time. We both liked the look of the MacGregor sailing yacht.

"Shall we buy it between us?" I asked. Mark agreed, and we signed a deal with the agent.

We couldn't wait to get it into the water. Neither of us had a clue about sailing. We were frightened to even put the sails up. We used the engine all the time, but had some great times out fishing and exploring the coastline over the next few years.

We called the boat "Michael's Gift" after our friend Michael Lord Castle, who had advised us on a deal. We ended up having a nice touch on the deal, so we named the boat after Micheal.

One morning, I was watching a TV programme about a young girl who took a boat like ours out sailing on her own.

"If she can do it, so can I," I thought.

So I got straight onto YouTube and sort of learned what to do — or so I thought. After a few hours of pulling ropes and canvas, I had the sails up — sort of — and off I went sailing out of the bay. I was really pleased with myself. We'd had that boat around two years and had never put the sails up. It was a lovely, sunny Mediterranean day, and as I left the bay, I put on a Johnny Cash album and had a beer.

"This is great," I thought. "I'm sailing alone!"

After a few beers or so, I must've fallen asleep listening to Johnny Cash, because the next thing I knew, I woke up to a strange noise. It must've been louder than the CD. I opened my eyes and looked around me.

"Jesus," I thought. "Where is Malta?"

I must've fallen asleep for a few hours. The boat had sailed on its own, because I could see no land, no coastline. Where was I?

The noise I'd heard was a large pod of dolphins playing around the boat. You couldn't make this up. The dolphins then left, so I quickly pulled down the sails. I put the engines on and headed in the same direction as them. I wasn't sure which way I was going.

After a few hours, I started to make out the coastline. I felt relieved — I must have drifted out a lot more than ten miles. All I had on was an old pair of shorts and a vest. It was starting to get cold, so I wrapped a towel around my chest. It was all I had on the boat.

When I eventually reached Birzebbuga harbour, it was dusk. The light was fading. If I'd been asleep any longer, God knows what would have happened.

After that scare, I made up my mind. I was going to get proper training and learn all I could about seamanship and navigation.

I found out that the Maltese government sponsored a course at the maritime institute in Kalkara. I enrolled in an RYA Yachtmaster Ocean course. It was a really intensive course, but I was really motivated to pass it.

In the class, there were about 25 guys, all Maltese. So most of the classes ended up being in Maltese. Although I had taken night classes learning Maltese, I was at a big disadvantage. But my enthusiasm and thirst for knowledge was a great equaliser.

The classes were four nights a week, three hours a night. It was very intensive, with a load of homework to go with it. We learned things like survival at sea, fire on board a ship, navigation, rules of the sea, and passage planning. It was all-encompassing. In the UK, this RYA course could take up to five years to achieve.

We had to take a monthly test on each module. You could fail a module, but not the navigation module.

Guess which module I failed?

My problem was that the instructor who taught us navigation was an Egyptian Maltese. I couldn't understand his accent. Even the other Maltese guys had problems understanding him. Before taking the exam, I knew I was struggling, and I went to the marine office to see if I could pay someone for private lessons in navigation. They couldn't help me.

What I didn't know was that our instructor was the director of the facility. That night, he asked me in front of the class why I had gone to the office asking for private lessons. So I explained to him — I'm the only non-Maltese here. I can't understand your accent, and I needed extra help. You should be helping me, not trying to make a show of me.

At the end of the course I had passed all the modules except the one I needed to pass. So I went to the port office again. I asked to take the test again. They told me I would have to take the whole course again next year. Just then, our instructor came out of his office when he heard the raised voices.

"You failed the test," he sneered.

"No, you failed." I replied.

He didn't understand.

"I was the only person in that whole course who never missed one lesson," I told him. "I was the only non-Maltese. I tried to get private lessons. I passed every other module. There wasn't another motivated student in that class. If I failed, you failed also."

He thought about it for a second, and relented, He told me I could take the navigation exam again in seven days' time.

Throughout the next week, I studied and studied. I practiced and practiced. I double-checked everything, because I assumed they wouldn't give me the same exam as before.

I was right. On the morning of the exam, I was very nervous, but the studying paid off. I passed with 98%. I couldn't believe it. I had earned an RYA Yachtmaster Ocean Certificate of Competence. This certificate is recognised and respected around the world. It is the ultimate aim of many skippers, both professional and recreational.

I sold Michael's Gift, and ended up buying a 40-foot Bavaria monohull yacht called *Sea Angel*. This was a much bigger boat than I had been used to, but I now had the confidence to go out on the open seas. Everything I was learning I was passing it on to Mary. We used to take the Sea Angel all around the Maltese Islands. We had some great times. We also made a lot of mistakes, but this was all part of the process.

One day, I suggested to Mary that we sail over to Lampedusa, an Italian island about 120 miles away between Malta and Tunisia.

"No problem," she said.

So we loaded up with provisions and headed out into the deep blue. Once the sun started going down and it started getting dark, the sea was a different place. I was very apprehensive but tried not to show it. We could see other ships because of their lights, but the fishermen laid lobster pots and you couldn't see them at night. It would be a real problem if they caught around our rudder or propeller.

Another thing we quickly learned was that not all fishermen use their lights at night. They were fishing illegally, so they turned off their navigational lights and tracking devices. If they turned everything off, you couldn't see them in the darkness. This could lead to some terrible accidents.

It must have been around 11 pm when we first saw the lights of Lampedusa. It was a big relief. Our first night passage was nearly over. We turned into port and found a lovely lit up bay with another four boats anchored there. This was going to be another first — anchoring at night. After some struggling, we got the hook down and breathed a huge sigh of relief. We had completed our first night passage and arrived safely. After a cup of tea, we went to bed.

Hours later, the boat shook violently.

"What's happening?" I thought. "Am I dreaming?"

I threw on a pair of shorts and went outside. It was just getting light. We had drifted and were now sitting on the rocks. Mary grabbed a rope, and we started waving and shouting to passing fishermen who were just leaving the bay to start a day's work.

They saw our problem and understood what had happened. They came close to us and threw us their rope. Mary attached it to the front of the Sea Angel, while I managed the helm and the engines. Luckily they pulled us at the same time as a big wave, and we came off the rocks without any damage.

After thanking them, we looked at each other. "Wow," we said. "We had a lucky escape there!"

It wouldn't be our last.

A month or two later, I suggested to Mary that we go a bit further and sail to Tunisia. It would take a couple of days of sailing and would be a big step up for us. We were both game for the adventure, as neither of us had been to Africa before.

So after planning a route and waiting for a good weather window, we set off for a port called Monastir. Most of the first day and night were uneventful, apart from when Mary spotted a whale on our starboard side. All you could see were these huge spurts of water coming out of the sea every few minutes. I steered the boat a bit closer for a better look, then used our binoculars to zoom in.

"Bloody hell, look at the size of that tail!" I shouted.

Without the binoculars, you couldn't see properly. When Mary saw the size of this thing, she panicked.

"Get out of here. NOW!"

I steered the boat away, and we never saw that whale again. Often, we would get dolphins and sea turtles around the boat. It was great to see them in their natural environment. But this was the only time we had seen a whale.

The next day, around 3 pm, I spotted the African Coast. We must have been around ten miles offshore. We had just passed some fish farms on our port side, sailing at a steady six knots. All of a sudden, the boat stopped dead in the sea.

We had hit a hidden sand bank. The sea was only about 2.5 feet deep ten miles out from shore. I wasn't too worried at first. I thought the waves would eventually wash us off the sandbank But after an hour or so, we still weren't moving. I knew I would have to do something.

I tied our anchor and the spare anchor to the end of the main boom and put the boom out mid-ship, hoping that the weight of the anchors would tilt us off the sandbank. But that didn't work. Luckily, Mary spotted some Tunisian fishermen. She started shouting and waving to them. They came over to help, but got stuck on the sandbank themselves.

The light was now starting to fade. Some of the fishermen got out of their boat and walked around their boat trying to push it off the sandbank. Unbelievable. I wish I had videoed it. Ten miles out at sea and walking in knee length water. Eventually, the fishermen got their boat off the sandbank. With some pulling of ropes, they got us off as well, but we had damaged our propeller and now needed a tow into the port at Monastir.

I could see that the fishermen weren't happy about having to give us a tow. They were going to lose a night's fishing. I talked to the captain in broken English and did a deal with him to tow us in. I gave the crew a bottle of whiskey that we had been told to bring for the custom guards in Tunisia.

About three hours later, we arrived in the port. I had learned my lesson. I was always looking above the water for obstructions and hadn't looked at the charts properly. Moving sandbanks were clearly marked, and I hadn't seen them.

Monastir was very different to what we had expected. The people were very friendly and helpful, but a lot of the infrastructure was like a third-world country. We soon adapted to our new surroundings and tried to blend in with the locals as much as possible. We realized how lucky we were living in a European country. These people had nothing, but they always had smiles on their faces. Sometimes, I think we all take too much for granted.

After exploring around the region for a week or so, we filled the tanks with some very cheap diesel and headed back eastwards towards Malta.

Some friends we met in Tunisia called us one morning and asked if we could call on a South African friend of theirs named Roger, who had a catamaran in a Maltese boatyard. He was undertaking some major repairs.

"No problem," I said, and we both headed off to Manoel Island Yacht Yard.

"You can't miss Roger's boat," our friends told us. They were right. It was a bright orange catamaran with a large South African flag fluttering from the stern.

We knocked on the hull of the boat. Roger appeared and called us onto the boat. After a cup of tea, he showed us around his boat.

Within minutes, I was hooked on the idea of a catamaran. It had so much more space, and Roger kept singing the praises of a catamaran over the monohull boat that we had.

"We're going to sell the Sea Angel and we're going to buy a Catamaran," I said to Mary.

In hindsight, if I had never have met Roger that day, I would have saved myself a small fortune.

From Belfast to Malta, Mary's family

Thats us moored up in Birzebuggia, Malta

21 | THE STARRY PLOUGH

I started at the computer screen for the next two weeks looking for the perfect catamaran. I scanned through all the boating and yacht websites looking for the ideal boat. After a lot of research and many phone calls, I found what I was looking for: a 41-foot Fountaine Pajot catamaran. It was berthed in La Rochelle, France.

My friend Paul Carr, Mary, and I flew over to La Rochelle to inspect the boat. Paul had a lifetime of experience on boats. After inspecting, we agreed a deal with the owner, subject to a marine surveyor inspecting her and a sea trail.

The boat passed all inspections. Now It was down to Mary and me to take the big cat out for a sea trail.

It was an early January morning when Mary and I left Malta to catch a flight to Paris. We made our way down to La Rochelle on the west coast of France. We assumed that the sea trail would go well. If it did, we would have to sail the cat 2,100 nautical miles — across the Bay of Biscay, down the Portuguese Atlantic Coast, through the Straits of Gibraltar into the Mediterranean Sea, and then across the Med to Malta.

We were full of excitement, but at the same time full of trepidation. Could we pull this off?

The sea trials went well. The boat was now ours. It was

like operating a 40-foot wagon and trailer, but on the water. I practiced maneuvering around the marina to get the hang of it. I did a deal with Didier, the owner, for him to sail across the Bay of Biscay with us to A Coruña in Spain. Everyone had advised against sailing across the notorious Bay Of Biscay in January. They all advised leaving it until June or July.

But I was keen to get going, so I took a calculated risk. We checked the weather hourly for two weeks until we found a good weather window to make the four-day dash across the Bay.

On that first night out on the bay, we had no idea what we were in for. Didier had been an Olympic sailor for France in his younger days and had lived his whole life on the Bay. 30-40 mph winds were a pleasant day out for him.

Meanwhile, Mary and I were shitting ourselves. We operated a three-hour watch system for the next four days, and although the first night was not what we were expecting, the next few days sailing across the Bay were okay. We were learning a lot from Didier.

After arriving in A Coruña, Didier left the boat. We were on our own. We provisioned up the boat and filled the tanks with diesel. We headed out into the Atlantic, just the two of us.

We had gotten used to what is called the Atlantic Swell. It was nothing like what we had been used to in the pleasant seas around Malta, but we were in charge of our own destiny. After about eight hours of sailing, we started to lose our Garmin maps on the chart plotter. The chart just disappeared from the screen.

It turned out later that Didier had only paid for charts north of the Bay of Biscay. As we sailed south of the Bay, the charts disappeared off the screen. Luckily, I had a backup on my iPad, and as we sailed passed Finisterre with clear open skies full of stars, we looked at each other and laughed. Here we were sailing along the Atlantic Coast of Spain heading towards Portugal. Just the two of us and miles and miles of nothing but clear vast skies ahead of us.

We had arranged to meet our friend Roger in Baiona in Portugal. He had taken pity on us and agreed to join us for the rest of the passage to Malta. Roger knew it was a dangerous crossing that we were undertaking. He knew that we were inexperienced and was keeping a close eye on us, and Mary and I very much appreciated him for it.

We sailed along the coast past Porto and Lisbon. The sailing was great, and we were making great headway with the winds behind us all the way. I suggested that we call into the port of Lagos just to walk on land again, as we had been on the boat for days now. We could also pick up some more provisioning.

That night, we ended up in a Portuguese cabaret restaurant. We had a great meal, and the wine was flowing.

It was great to release some of the anxiety and tension that builds up when you are out at sea on your own. It's different on a cruise ship with lots of people around and staff who know what they are doing. It's completely different when you are literally three feet above the water in the darkness with the winds howling around you.

It's not a natural space to be in. It's hard to explain to someone who hasn't experienced it.

After leaving Lagos, we sailed around the southern tip of Portugal past Albufeira and Cádiz and through the Straits of Gibraltar. Going through the straits was a strange experience. You have Africa to your starboard side and Europe on your port side, with only seven miles of distance between them. You also need to be aware of the strong tides and the almost continuous stream of container ships, tankers, recreational crafts, and God knows what else.

After going through the Straits, we were in the Med. Somehow, I sort of missed the giant Atlantic Swell that we had become used to. If we thought it was easy sailing from here on in, we were about to get a rude awakening.

Every night after dinner around 7 pm, we would start our nighty three-hour shift. Each person kept watch for three hours, which meant you should get at least six hours of sleep each night.

On the first night in the Med, Roger was at the helm steering the boat. I was in the galley cleaning up after dinner, and Mary was sleeping downstairs. Suddenly, out of nowhere, a rogue wave washed over the boat. The weight of the wave dragged the boat down further into the sea.

Alarms were going off everywhere. Everything was in complete darkness. The wave had come over the back of the boat. I was waist-high in sea water. I tried to get down the stairs to wake Mary, but she felt the wave right away and was trying to get out of the bed. The sea water was all around her knees.

"What happened?" She shouted to me.

I didn't know. I started climbing the stairs to go up to the helm station, when Roger came down to meet us. The alarms were still ringing. But it was all over in about a minute.

"What just happened, Roger?" I asked.

"No problem," he said, cool as you like. "We just got pooped."

"What do you mean we just got fuckin' pooped?" I was incredulous.

Apparently, this was a nautical term for when a huge wave unexpectedly washed over a boat. It was a hell of an experience. I don't know about Roger, but Mary and I didn't sleep a wink that night.

A few days later, we stopped for some provisions in Ibiza. We stayed overnight, and the next morning headed for Sardinia. We only stayed in Sardinia for about six hours, just enough time to refuel the boat and grab a bite to eat. Off we went towards Tunisia, arriving there about three days later. We hung around the port in Tunisia for a few days rest and then set sail for Malta, arriving two days later.

Apart from the pooping, we'd had no real drama since leaving the Bay of Biscay about a month before. Roger played a big part in that. His easy way and gentle guidance made the trip really enjoyable, and we learned so much from him. For that, we will be eternally grateful to Roger.

In a lot of ways, it was great to be back home in Malta. We had missed our friends and the social life. The island has this sort of magical draw that keeps you returning.

Earlier, we had joined a group called The Malta Cruisers. We really enjoyed the company and comradeship that came from this group of like-minded people who owned boats from around the island. The group organised cruises to different Mediterranean spots. There was a good social scene as well with BBQ nights and pub quizzes. There was also a good selection of practical demonstrations, which always finished with a few beers and a good meal.

In late April, we received an invite to attend a yearly meeting of Fountaine Pajot owners at an isolated island on the southern coast of France called Porquerolles. I had never heard of this place before, but I jumped at the opportunity to sail up to southern France. A few weeks later, we were on our way again.

We called in at the Italian island of Pantelleria on the way. It lies 50 miles south of Sicily. We climbed to the top of the mountain on the island. It is said that on a clear day, you can see Sicily to the west and Africa to the east. We only stayed a few days before setting off towards Sardinia and a place called Porto Corallo. We hired a car and drove around sightseeing the southeast of Sardinia, which was great to discover.

Our next stop was Porto-Vecchio in Corsica, which was around 130 miles north. After a few hours sailing, the winds started to build, but nothing that alarmed us.

I knew that around 2 am we would have to sail across the famous Bonifacio Pass, a six-mile-wide stretch of water that separates Sardinia from Corsica. The Pass could generate some terrible currents. It was a graveyard for many sailors over the years. So that night, we would both be on watch all night.

As darkness fell, the winds built up to around a force six. This always seemed to happen to us as soon as it got dark. I kept a close watch on the AIS tracker for other traffic. There was plenty about tonight. During night sailing, you are always on the lookout for lights. This is the most effective way of knowing what other crafts are out there.

Maritime law states that there should only be three colours of light used: green for starboard, red for port, and white as a stern anchoring light. The theory is that by seeing a green, red, or white light around you, it's possible to determine which way another craft is heading.

This particular night, with the force six blowing around us, what I wasn't expecting to see was yellow, purple, pink, orange lights — every colour of the rainbow, it seemed — right in front of us. I checked the AIS. It was a bloody big cruise ship heading straight for us.

I tried to call him on the VHF, but got no reply, so I tacked our boat to port. He seemed to be going to port also, so I tacked to Starboard, and he seemed to be turning to starboard now also. I tried calling him again on the VHF. No answer.

"Are they all asleep on the bridge?" I said to Mary.

Things were happening really quickly now. He was less than a mile from us, which is nothing when these cruise ships were going 20 knots. We dropped our sails totally now, and I turned the boat towards the coast.

The big white thing passed us by, but only just.

"That's it, Mary," I said. "I'm heading way out to sea."

What I had been doing was keeping as close to the shore as was safe, using the cliffs and the shoreline as cover from the wind. By going offshore, we were exposing ourselves more to the elements, but I didn't want any more encounters with cruise ships.

That night we counted eight cruise ships. What I now know is that all the cruise ships use the Bonifacio Pass as a shortcut between Sardinia and Corsica instead of going around the islands on their way to Rome on the Italian mainland.

Local knowledge is a great thing, and every day on the sea you learn something. The next afternoon we arrived in Porto-Vecchio. After registering with the harbour master, we went straight to bed. We were knackered from the lack of sleep the previous night.

After spending the next day looking around the old town, we decided to keep moving. I set the autopilot for Bastia around 70 miles north at the top finger of Corsica. It was a beautiful day, perfect for sailing. We had a nice lunch and a bit of a kip on the deck.

After a few hours, our VHF crackled to life. There was a guy calling out our boat's name.

"Starry Plough, Starry Plough."

I picked up the handset. "This is the Starry Plough."

"This is the Italian Coast Guard," the voice said. "Turn 90 degrees immediately. You have sailed into restricted waters. This area is a live war games area."

Whoops. We had watched these fighter aircrafts flying above us for hours. In fact, I had seen them the day before. I immediately turned 90 degrees to our port and put both engines on full throttle.

Once I was outside the coordinates that the Coast Guard gave me, we relaxed. We put the sails back up and carried on northwards towards Bastia. It must've been about an hour later that Mary pointed.

"There's a warship over there," she said.

I assumed that it was part of the war games and didn't take a lot of notice. About fifteen minutes later, I got a call on the VHF.

"This is the Italian Navy," the voice said.

The warship was now almost on top of us, circling

around the boat. I stopped the engines. The guy on the VHF spoke once more.

What is your destination?" He asked. "What was your last port of call? How many are on board?"

I answered him. After a few minutes of silence, he spoke again.

"This boat is SSR registered," he said. "It's a UK boat? Why no UK flag?"

"Let me explain," I told him. "It may be UK registered, but this is an Irish boat, and the only flag going on this boat is an Irish Tricolour."

We heard them laughing in the background.

"Ok, sir. Carry on."

We have always flown the Irish Tricolour on all our boats. Many harbour masters have asked me the same question about the flag. They always get the same answer.

"Well, that's enough excitement for one day, Mary!" I laughed as we turned on the engines and headed for Bastia.

I could see before arriving that this was a busy port. There were ferries coming from every direction, but mostly from mainland France. We kept away from the commercial end of the port and found a quiet spot on a pontoon. The town itself was ancient, with a large cathedral overlooking the old town. We went for a beer in one of the many restaurants along the quay. We spent the next few days just lazily discovering the old town and making plans to sail across to Porquerolles.

The island of Porquerolles is the largest of three islands in an area known as Hyères on the French Riviera. We had never heard of it before, but our friends and the other catamaran owners had agreed to meet there for their yearly get-together.

The island itself is beautiful, and with less than 200 people living there it was very exclusive. There are no cars on the island — you either walk everywhere or hire a bike. It is also a nature park, with a lot of restrictions to maintain its beauty.

There were around 30 catamarans there when we arrived. We had a fantastic week on the island. Everything was very well-organised, with boat races every day followed by a BBQ on a remote beach. One night, they arranged a gala dinner at the only winery on the island. Most nights, we all ended up in the small town square, drinking beer and wine while having a singsong between around twenty different nationalities.

After a week of this we were all ready for a rest. As the other catamarans sailed away to all four corners, Mary and I sailed four miles to a small, deserted island called Port-Cros. Port-Cros is an uninhabited island, with no cars or even bikes. You had to walk everywhere. We loved the place — we felt just like Robison Crusoe.

On the second day there, I said, "Let's climb the mountain." So off we set.

The place was just like a jungle. There were animal

noises everywhere. The sun was beating down, but under the canopy of all the trees and bushes it was almost dark. It took us about two hours to reach the top of the mountain. As we reached the top, a giant snake slithered in front of us.

It may have taken two hours to trek up the mountain, but after seeing that snake, it only took us two minutes to get back down.

After a few days of rest on Port-Cros, we were unsure of what to do next. Should we head back to Malta? Sail to Greece? Sail to Spain? We had unlimited choices.

I read that Formula One would be in Monaco the following week. Monaco was only 70 miles away, so we lifted anchor and started sailing slowly up the French Riviera.

We stopped in Saint-Tropez and Nice along the way. These weren't really our scene. We thought they were full of posers. If it wasn't for the F1, we would have headed south away from the French coast altogether.

As we approached Monaco, we had to be impressed by the mega yachts. The biggest yachts in the world were anchored all around us. We must have looked out of place in our tiny Cat as we maneuvered between them.

I motored away from all the madness over to the far side of the bay, and we anchored off a secluded beach for the night. The next morning, we took our dinghy ashore to have a look at Monte Carlo. The place was dripping in wealth and money. Every car was a Rolls Royce, Ferrari, or

Lamborghini...not exactly what we were used to.

I couldn't wait to get out of that place. I even saw a shop that was selling private aeroplanes. Just like a normal grocer that we're used to, but they were selling aeroplanes.

We went back to the boat for lunch. No way was I paying these fancy prices. That night, we went out walking along the F1 course, just people watching. There was a fantastic atmosphere and excitement about the whole place. There were hundreds of massive yachts moored along each other, and every second one seemed to have a live band on them.

That night, there was an open-air disco on the finish line. Thousands of people were dancing and singing. It was good to experience it, but also good to leave it.

The next morning was race day. The noise from the cars was deafening. We didn't have tickets for the race, and the officials had put hoarding up around the whole course. Along with thousands of others, we watched the race on a big screen, with the cars flying past us six feet away.

I can't remember who won. It was good to experience it, but I won't be rushing back.

At first light the next morning, we lifted the anchor and sailed up the coast. We weren't looking for anywhere in particular. Just wherever the wind took us.

We ended up in a place called San Remo right on the French/Italian border. Once we moored in the marina, I Googled the place and found that there was a cycle track running along the coast following an old railway line. It went for 24 km along the coast. We took our bikes off the boat and went and did the ride.

It couldn't have been more different from the day before, with all the noise from the F1. Now, as we cycled along the coast on a beautiful day, we were in heaven. We stopped for lunch at a small shack. In the afternoon, we slowly made our way back up the track to the boat.

I looked at the charts in the morning to see what was next on the agenda. We talked about following the Italian coast down to Rome 250 miles away. Then, I saw Elba on the map. I remembered reading that Elba was the island that Napoleon had been exiled to. It was only 120 miles away, halfway between San Remo and Rome. We could do a night shift and be there sometime tomorrow afternoon.

The sail down to Elba was fantastic. The wind was behind us the whole way, so we used our spinnaker. That night, we had a full moon. Nights like that are unbelievable — the whole sea was lit up before us, and it was still about 25 degrees through the night.

In the morning, before the sun had risen, we could see the cliffs of Elba in the distance. We moored in the main town of Portoferraio. This was a very pleasant place — so easygoing, and the people were very friendly.

There was a lot to see on Elba, so after a few days in Portoferraio, we sailed around to the other side of the island and dropped our anchor in Golfo di Campo in about six feet of water. The beach there was just off a postcard. We swam to the beach from the boat with a drybag and had lunch and a few beers.

"It doesn't get any better than this," I thought.

After a day or so, it was time to lift the hook again. This time, we were heading for Rome. Since we left Malta weeks before, we never stayed anywhere apart from Porquerolles for more than a few days. There was just so much to see. I had been to Rome a few times before, but Mary had never been there and was very excited to see the Vatican.

We arrived in the Marina Di Roma a few days later. This was a massive marina situated about ten miles outside the capital. We had to get a bus to the train station, then a train into Rome, and then the metro to get around the city.

We went to all the usual places — The Pantheon, The Colosseum, Trevi Fountain, The Spanish Steps, but our favourite place was the Vatican. We spent two whole days there, and I still don't think we saw half of it.

Back at the marina, a guy came up to us on the boat.

"Is this an Irish Boat?" He asked.

"Yes, mate," I replied.

He introduced himself. his name was James,and he was a pilot for EasyJet. He lived on a boat full time in the Marina di Roma with his girlfriend Louise and her cat. He came from an Irish background and had seen the Tricolour flying from our boat.

We welcomed him and Louise aboard for a beer. After a few hours of exchanging stories over beers, Louise had to go back to her boat. She explained that their cat was called Bailey Cat, and that Bailey Cat had to make an internet appearance every day at certain times. Apparently, Bailey Cat had over 10,000 followers on the social media, with many of these followers paying money to speak to the cat every day.

We couldn't believe it. James and Louise were making a lot more money with Bailey Cat than from his wages from Easyjet.

We stayed for a week in Rome and then sailed south. I suggested to Mary that we should sail over to Greece. We could take a shortcut through the Strait of Messina between Sicily and the Italian mainland and then sail across from the mainland to Corfu. I wanted to stop at a small island on the way called Lipari, which is the largest of the Aeolian Islands just north of Sicily.

Our boat was a Fountaine Pajot Lipari, and I thought we should see this island that our boat was named after. On the second morning after leaving Rome, I awoke to see Stromboli right in front of me. Mary was just finishing the 3 am-6 am shift. As I climbed to the helm station to take the wheel, I marvelled at the huge volcano of Stromboli. She is one of the only active volcanoes in the world. Smoke was rising from her peak as we passed. Stromboli is really impressive and stands over 3000 feet above sea level.

Unbelievably, around 500 people live at the foot of the volcano. We were half a mile away on the boat, and we could still smell the Sulphur from there.

As we passed Stromboli, Lipari and the rest of the Aeolian Islands came into sight. We moored in Marina Lunga in the main town of Lipari. Just our luck, Ireland were playing Italy that night in the Euros. That night, as we made our way into the main town, the place was heaving. Italy was at home. The whole town had come into the main street to watch the football, and there was Mary and myself with Irish tops on in the middle of all these jumping Italians.

Well, the craic was 90. They were all very good-humoured, and as Robbie Brady scored the winner for us with five minutes to go. We both jumped into the air. You could have heard a pin drop. Everyone was looking at us, but I didn't give a monkey's. We were hopping about the main street like two demented eejits.

It was one of them moments. In fact, some of the Italians came over to us at the end wanting to shake our hands and buy us a drink.

The next morning, the main street was back to normal business. After breakfast, we travelled around the island on our bikes to have a good look at the place.

"Well, that's Lipari, and fair play to the Irish!" I thought as we left the jetty and sailed off in the direction of the Strait of Messina.

As we approached the straits, we noticed these strange-looking boats. They were fishing boats, but they had a lookout/spotter about 40 feet up in the air in a crow's nest. They also had a guy with a harpoon on a sort of a drawbridge 30 feet out in front of the boat.

These boats were specifically designed for catching swordfish. The swordfish spends much of its time in deep ocean waters, coming to the warmer, shallower waters around the Strait of Messina from May to August to mate. We were lucky to see all the action right in front of us. There were four boats involved, and although we couldn't see the swordfish, we could follow all the action as the four boats closed in on the giant fish.

Guided by the spotters in the lookout nest, they caught the fish after a 30-minute chase. It seemed that they have been fishing this way for hundreds of years.

Going through the Strait of Messina for the first time, I wondered what all the fuss was about, as we had heard many horror stories about the straits and so we lowered our main sail as a precaution and just used the genoa. There was a lot of traffic in the straits criss crossing from Sicily to the mainland and going up and down the straits like us. We were apprehensive as we approached. The wind speed was around 8-10 knots.

Within seconds, our wind speed sensor shot up to 28 knots. The boat just took off. It was great because the wind was at our back. Within minutes, we were through the straits. We were meant to turn to port at the end of the straits to head for Corfu, but we decided to go with the wind.

We carried on sailing for about three hrs until we reached Taormina 25 miles down the coast.

That night, we dropped the anchor in the bay at the bottom of the hill that leads up to the village of Taormina. In the morning, we took a local bus up the mountain to the village. The views were spectacular. You could see why tourists flocked to this place and why so many films were made here. We spent the day walking all around the village and had dinner that night at a mountainside restaurant with views out across the Mediterranean. We really appreciated our surroundings and the life we were living.

After breakfast in the morning, we raised both sails and headed off towards Corfu and Greece. If we got the right winds, we would get there in about 2.5 days. The trip over was mostly uneventful. The seas and the winds played their part, and we arrived on the west coast of Corfu at a place called Ormos Liapades just before darkness. We found somewhere to anchor and started to prepare dinner.

Mary and I had a system on the boat. I would do the cooking and she would do the cleaning. Mostly, we ate on the boat. Although there were many great restaurants we saw on all our travels, we preferred home cooking over eating out. Even if the food was free in the restaurants we would prefer home cooking any day of the week.

The next morning, we had a leisurely sail around the top of Corfu heading for the main town. As we rounded the northeast corner of the island, we were less than two miles from Albania, and we were tempted to call there and have a look. After everything I had read about the place, we decided to give it a miss. An hour or so later, we docked on the quayside right in the middle of Corfu Town.

The old town itself had loads of character, and again the people were really friendly, but you could see how the place had lost some of its charm to the thousands of tourists that flock there. We stayed a few days on that quayside, and no one came near us for payment, which was very unusual. In other countries, the marine or port officials were straight over to you for your passport and payment. We spent the next month in Greece, and not once were we asked for payment from anyone.

Of all the countries we travelled in around the Mediterranean, we loved Greece the most. the sailing and the scenery were just spectacular, and it was cheap to live there. We travelled to so many islands — it's impossible to name then all.

Our favourite place was Vonitsa, this hidden little gem in an inland sea. If we hadn't been told about it by some friends, you would never know it was there. It was like going back in time 50 years.

After leaving Vonitsa, we passed by Preveza and sailed through the Lefkas Canal, stopping at Kefalonia and heading into the Gulf of Patras. This gulf was around 70 miles long, and as we sailed its length towards the Corinth Canal we saw bushfires on the hills leading down the shore.

The weather was so hot that most of the countryside that we sailed passed on the bay was burnt to a cinder. At night, you could really see the flames and the fire brigades fighting the fires.

At the end of this very long gulf was the Corinth Canal. This man-made canal cuts right through the Mani Peninsula separating the Peloponnese from the Greek mainland and the Ionian Sea from the Aegean Sea. There are no locks on the canal and it is about four miles long.

As you sail through the canal in a convoy, you have to be impressed by the manpower that built this without modern machinery. The walls are up to 300 feet high either side, and it is only 80 feet wide. All the rock was cut by hand. I don't know how some of these huge tankers got through.

We motored through the narrow strip at about three knots, and I was sorry when we got to the other end. After working in construction all my life, I really appreciated what these men that built this had achieved.

Once through the canal, although you are still in Greece, you can really notice the difference between the Ionian Sea and the Aegean Sea. We preferred the Ionian any day. It was so much cleaner and quieter. Here in the Aegean, the sea traffic was very busy. There were high-speed ferries called flying dolphins, and every few minutes they crisscrossed in front of us and behind us on their way from the islands to the main port in Athens.

We stayed in Athens for a week or so. Its long maritime

history was everywhere, but after a few days looking around all the sights of the city, I was happy to leave it behind us and head out to the dozens of islands in front of us. We slowly made our way to through the islands to Kythira, where we had agreed to meet our friend Roger, who was sailing the Greek islands himself that summer.

We spent a few days together with Roger in Kythira. Because it was getting towards the end of September, we needed to make our way back to Malta before the winter storms came. Roger was heading to Rhodes for the winter, the opposite way from us, so we provisioned the boat, filled it with fuel, and said our goodbyes to Roger and to Greece. What a trip it had been!

It would take us four days and nights to sail from Greece to Malta. Luckily, I had picked the right weather window. The sail back was largely uneventful, apart from the third night out. During the day, we had heard a message over the VHF from a British warship out on patrol. These waters we were sailing through were notorious for smugglers and immigrants trying to get from Libya to Europe. There was a lot of fuel smuggling out of Libya, and the European military patrolled the seas looking for bandits.

At about 2am, I was on watch. I thought I saw a big black thing in front of me. I woke Mary so she could have a look, because sometimes at night, your eyes can play tricks on you. I wanted a second opinion. We thought it was something noteworthy, but we didn't know what.

I dropped the sails and went under the engines very slowly. What was it?

It was a bloody great big tanker. The bugger had turned off his lights and his AIS. They were a mothership smuggling fuel to smaller ships that would rendezvous with them at a given point. We had almost sailed straight into them. We were literally only a few yards apart when we properly made out the shape of the ship.

I thought about calling the warship on the VHF and giving the ship's coordinates. But this ship would be listening on the VHF for any vocal traffic, and if they hear us talking and start shooting, we'd be sunk before anyone ever found us.

So we carried on towards Malta. After about 30 mins, we were still talking about what had happened. The lights of the ship came on behind us. I checked the AIS, and sure enough, there it was on the screen.

We had a lucky escape that night. We were only minutes away from sailing straight into the ghost.

All of 2016, after picking up the boat in January at La Rochelle in France, we had sailed down the Atlantic and around most of the Mediterranean. In the process, we had travelled a total of 6,500 nautical miles. We saw some unbelievable places, met some unbelievable people, and made some unbelievable mistakes on the boat.

But we had learned so much. Not just about sailing, but about ourselves as well. What a year!

The Starry Plough, we seen a lot with the old girl

A sword-fishing boat at the Messina straits near Sicily

22 | A BOXING LOVE AFFAIR

Boxing has been a big part of my life from an early age. As I said earlier, my Ma first took me and Seamus to the old St. John Bosco Club in Belfast at around 8 years old. When we first joined Crawley Amateur Boxing Club, the coaches at that time were Dave Baldry and Dick Hardwick, with Maurice Tyson doing the matchmaking.

Usually, before we youngsters started, the pros were just finishing. It was great to see someone like Alan Minter, undisputed World Middleweight Champion, cooling down after a session. It always gave us something to look up to.

The other senior fighters I remember from that time were Clint Jones, Micky Minter, John Flynn, John Pincham, and Sean Chalcraft.

We trained and boxed right through our teenage years. I remember that I couldn't get enough of it. At Crawley, we trained Monday, Wednesday and Friday, so I joined another club to fill in the gaps. At the Crawley Boys Club, under coaches Tony Gunning and Pat Nelson, we trained Tuesday, Thursday, and Saturday morning, I just loved it, and I never told either club that I was going to the other.

I think that boxing is a great leveler in life. It teaches discipline, routine, comradeship, and many other benefits that kids just don't seem to have these days.

At school, we also had a boxing club, and we all boxed in the schoolboy championships. I cannot understand why boxing is not taught at schools these days. It would certainly do away with all the knife crime that we have today with teenagers.

After leaving school, I carried on the training for many years. It was only really when the business started taking off that I just couldn't find the time I needed to go down to the gym.

At the Crawley Club, they have a really dedicated team of coaches — people like Keith Gabriel, Paddy Harmey, Rees and Peter Hopcraft, Paul Devlin, and Peter Charlton. The amount of time that these guys give to the club is never really appreciated and noticed. There's well over a century of experience between them, and I would just like to say a big thank you for all their efforts.

George Brown was another great servant of Crawley for many years.

In later years, as a business, we started supporting the Crawley Club, with sponsorships and selling tickets for upcoming amateur shows. In 2006, I had the great pleasure of being asked to become the club's president, taking over from Alan Minter, who had been president for the previous two years. Fourteen years later, it's still a great privilege to be president of the club.

In 2008, the committee of the club at that time — Rees and Peter Hopcraft, Geoff Hopcraft, George Brown, Paddy

Harmey, Shirley Pearce, the old man, and I — decided that because of the success that the club was having and the number of young lads that the club was attracting, we needed to build an extension to the club. I was assigned the task of finding the funding and then building it.

I quickly attained charitable status for the club, with myself and Paddy Harmey becoming the two trustees. This status would enable us to obtain grants and funding.

Finding funding was a hard task at first. At the time, Sports England had allocated all funding for the forthcoming London Olympics and told us that we had no chance of getting lottery funding. Undeterred, we persevered. After a lot of bartering, haggling, and — in the end — threatening to go to the press because the lottery money should have been for all charities, not just the London Olympics, we received a grant for £250,000.

Brian Quinn, the lord mayor of Crawley at that time and a good friend, really helped the club as well. He helped show me where we could obtain funding. It wasn't long before we had all the funds needed to rebuild the club and car park.

Alan Minter and the new lord mayor of Crawley Laura Moffatt jointly cut the ribbon to the new club. It was brilliant to see a lot of the old boxers from the club's past 30 years turn up, and we certainly had a good drink in the Conservative Club next door to celebrate.

It must have been around 2005. I would have been 45 years old when I heard about this new organisation in

London called "The Real Right Club" where business people from different backgrounds boxed each other over three two-minute rounds in packed halls and hotels in London. I thought I'd give it. I had no idea what I was getting myself into. Boxing is a young man's game, and I was just about to learn that lesson the hard way.

I used to train at the Kronk Gym in Kentish Town, London. They had some retired pros there training with us, including Errol Christie and Spencer Fearon. The training and sparring was good, but travelling up to the Kronk everyday just took so much time. So I contacted Barry McGuigan, who had recently opened our new offices, and he put me in contact with Ronnie Davis, Chris Eubanks's old trainer down in Brighton.

Ronnie only agreed to train me as a favor to Barry. He said he couldn't do the corner, as the Board of Control did not approve of this unlicensed boxing. So every day, I went down to his basement club in Hove to train for this upcoming fight. They didn't really give me much quarter. You trained just like all the young pros in the gym, but they took it easy on me in the sparring.

I made some great friends there, and one guy named Neil Linford — who fought Tony Oakey for the World Light Heavyweight Title later that year — was very helpful in giving me tips and sparring. Later, he worked for the company for a while.

After a few months of training with Ronnie, I was due to

fight a white South African guy at the Royal National Hotel in London. I was very confident going in after all the training and sparring I had done.

I was surprised at the weigh-in when I met my opponent and he told me he had come from Johannesburg just for this fight. I was sure I'd been set up. There was a crowd of around 1,000 people there. Everyone from my office was there, so the pressure was really on.

Luckily, I knocked the guy out in the first round. What a relief!

My next bout was arranged for around eight weeks' time, so it was back down to Ronnie's gym in Hove for more heartache. This time, the fight was back in the same hotel, and the guy was about fifteen years younger than me. After three hard rounds, they called the fight a draw, but I knew I had lost it. I was just too old for this game. So I went back to the administration side of the game with my old club Crawley.

I'll leave the fighting to the young guys.

NEWS Sport

A DATE FOR THE FOREMAN

Our next Foreman and Contract Managers meeting has been confirmed for Friday November 22 at 7pm. The meeting will be held at the Gatwick Worth Hotel and drinks will be served in the bar afterwards.

LEN DELIVERS FIRST ROUND KNOCKOUT!

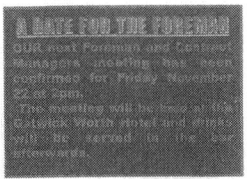

NEARLY 20 years since hanging up his gloves Len Nugent has ducked the ropes again and joined the Real Fight Club.

South African blasted out

By **Mark Schneidau**

Despite not lacing up a pair of gloves in all those years Len's love of the sport saw him make a belated comeback to the ring at London's Royal National Hotel.

Boxing under the rules of the International White Collar Boxing Association, Len soon got back into the swing of things as he blasted his way to a sensational first round knockout.

South African mine owner Pete 'The Drill' Beldenko had flown over to London for the fight only to suffer a savage beating.

In front of the BBC cameras Len gave the waiting crowd the fireworks they had been waiting for.

After teeing up the South African with a couple of jabs a big shot exploded on to Beldenko's chin sending him crashing to the canvas.

The Real Fight Club gives weary desk bound businessmen and executives the chance to do battle with their peers under the rules of the noble art.

The organisation, which raises money for charity, began 12 years ago in New York and has now grown across the globe to Hong Kong, Frankfurt, Dublin and London.

Len is now back in the gym getting ready for his next outing on October 24.

Anyone one who fancies watching the boss in action can contact the office for tickets.

KNUCKLES NUGENT after his first round knockout of Peter Beldenko

From left hooks to boat hooks

AWAY from the real mans world of the fight game the Nugent group took to the Solent recently for a spot of sailing.

A fine June day saw six 40 foot Sunsail yachts, crewed by a selection of site foreman, management and clients along with a Sunsail skipper.

After a bellyful of hot coffee and bacon rolls the yachts sailed gently out of Port Solent and into the deep clear water as they made their way to an anchor point close to Cowes, Isle of Wight for a spot of lunch.

Following a top up of prawns and champers the race was on to navigate a course set over the radio.

Pat O'Dwyers team of novices rolled in first and after a well earned drink at the bar trophies were awarded after dinner, with Group Managing Director Len Nugent taking great pleasure in awarding Mark Schneidau and his team of golden oldies the wooden spoon.

The hard training paid off

The Crawley boxing squad in Cyprus, 2006

Still hitting the bag at 60!

23 | THE ATLANTIC DREAM

After our long sail around the Mediterranean in 2016, I talked to Mary about one day sailing across the Atlantic Ocean. The 6,000 nautical miles of sailing that we had done had given us some confidence in our own seamanship skills. But an ocean was a different beast altogether.

For the next couple of years, I started to do my research on the Atlantic. I read every book I could get my hands on and watched numerous videos and films. We went to various seminars in the UK and took a meteorologist course so we could understand cloud formations and weather patterns. We also took first aid courses. We wanted to be well-prepared, and we left no stone unturned.

Next, I turned my attention to the boat. We would need to upgrade some stuff and add some new things. First, I added a new radar system and a new AIS tracker. After that, we added a Hydrovane, which would give us a secondary rudder if required and a secondary steering system if our autopilot broke. Next we added a hydro-generator, which would enable us to generate extra power to the batteries.

Next on the list was a reverse osmosis unit, which would enable us to make our own water straight from the sea. We updated the chart plotter and added an Iridium Go WiFi system, which would enable us to download the weather from anywhere on earth. It also acted as a satellite phone. Next, we added a fuel-polishing system to make sure our fuel was always clean. We also painted the bottom of the hull in copper-coating so that we didn't attract any seaweed and growth that would slow us down. Lastly, we upgraded our sails and rigging.

We probably spent in excess of £30,000 to prepare the boat. Carrying out all this work took time, but we were hoping to leave after the summer in Malta.

On September 24th, 2019, we said all of our goodbyes to friends and family and set off from Malta to cross the Atlantic. Our plan was to sail the first 1,000 miles across the Mediterranean to Gibraltar, then catch the trade winds down to the Canary Islands to provision the boat. We'd continue on across the Atlantic sailing on the trade winds, arriving in the Caribbean sometime around the end of January 2020.

When we left the quay at Birzebbuga that Tuesday morning, our plan for a lazy sail up to Gnejna Bay in the north of the island. But from that first day, the predicted winds did not do as promised. We arrived late in the afternoon and dropped anchor in the secluded bay.

Originally, our plan was to leave early the next morning, but the wind was against us. So we waited in the bay for a few days until we got a clear weather window. Our next destination was Monastir in Tunisia, which was around 180 miles to our west.

Soon enough, the winds changed, and we were off. We had fantastic blue skies almost all day. Just before dark, I cooked dinner. After dinner, our routine was to check all the sails, and we started a three hours on, three hours off shift pattern.

With only Mary and I on the boat, someone always had to be at the helm looking out for fishing boats, other pleasure crafts, tankers, cargo vessels, and everything in between. Many times, we had hairy experiences with fishermen trawling nets at night without lights because they were illegally fishing.

That night was a quiet one. Around midnight, we sailed through the channel between Lampedusa and Linosa, the two Italian islands at the southernmost tip of Europe.

We are always very aware when in these waters, as this is where most of the illegal immigrants leaving Libya and North Africa head for. We have stopped a few times in the past at Lampedusa, but were never impressed by the place. There has been very little investment there by the Italian authorities, and it shows in the building and infrastructure on the island.

In the early hours of the morning, we passed from European waters into Tunisian waters. We hoisted our Tunisian courtesy flag. We headed north around the small island of Kurat along about ten miles of the Tunisian coast and Monastir. It's a bit longer this way, but this was the place a few years earlier where we got caught on the shifting sandbank. Now, I was ultra-careful sailing in these waters. As we approached the shore, the minaret of the main mosque in the town stood out from the rest of the buildings, and you could actually hear the chants of the calling to prayers.

We stayed in the marina in Monastir for around a week doing some small jobs on the boat. We filled up the tanks and some fuel containers that we had brought along with diesel. The diesel in Tunisia was really cheap. In fact, most things were a quarter of the price in Europe. After waiting for a few days for the right weather window, we headed off north out of Monastir, across the Gulf of Hammamet and up towards Sardinia.

This passage meant we had to cross one of the main shipping lanes in the Mediterranean just north of Tunis. As we approached the shipping lanes, we were engulfed in a massive squall. Within minutes, we were drenched, as the torrential rain came from nowhere. The wind jumped from a steady 15 knots to over 40 knots.

It was all hands on deck as we struggled to drop our main sail to take some of the wind's power away from the sails. We had been caught in big squalls before, but always in daylight. At night, with all the darkness around us, we couldn't see these squalls approaching. This one came from nowhere, and it didn't register on our radar before it hit us.

We managed to get the main sail down and tried to steady the boat as the waves — which were now up around

2+ meters high — battered the side of our port hull. I was very conscious of the tankers and container ships in the shipping lanes beside us, and engaged both engines to try and steer ourselves away from the danger.

After an hour or so, our prayers were answered, and the winds died to around 20 knots. I re-tightened the front genoa sail to give the boat some balance. We got our bearings back and headed off into the darkness, praying for no more squalls.

The rest of the night was quiet as we passed through the shipping lanes. As the sun rose the next morning, we were about halfway to Sardinia.

Around lunchtime that same day, the sea was calm and we were making good time. We had just had something to eat, when all of a sudden, we started noticing millions and millions of flies around the boat. They were dying on the deck, literally dying like flies.

We quickly closed all the hatches and portholes, but the whole boat was covered in dead flies. This went on all afternoon. We had never seen anything like it before. We were 75 miles offshore. Where were they coming from? There was nothing else around us, but these flies just fell out of the sky. We cleaned the top of the deck again and again, but still they dropped on us. It was only when darkness fell that night that they stopped.

The rest of the night was uneventful, and Mary and I swapped shifts every three hours. In the morning, there were no more flies. Whatever had been left had been washed away by the odd wave that crashed over our bow. Now, as the light started to appear for a new day, we could see the cliffs of southern Sardinia about twelve miles ahead of us. After downloading the weather forecast I decided to head for a small hidden port called Carloforte on the island of San Pietro, just off the southern coast of Sardinia.

There was a cold front coming through, and this small port allowed us to hide up out of the way until the front passed. We ended up staying in Carloforte for a week because the weather never got any better. We had walked all around the island a number of times during that week just to pass the time and to keep fit. But after a week, I was restless.

"Let's take a chance," I said to Mary. "And make a break for Menorca."

Menorca was just over 200 miles away and on our route to Gibraltar. It would take an overnight passage to get there, and it brought us closer to the Atlantic. So the next morning, after checking the weather again, we set off. The forecast wasn't great. There were storms due the next day, but I reckoned that if we were lucky, we could just about make it to Menorca.

So off we set in a brisk 18-20 knots on our beam. Most of that day was uneventful, and there was another yacht that left San Pietro about the same time as us. He was about five miles to our starboard as I followed him on the AIS. Just before dusk, I called the skipper of this boat. It was called Taloa on the VHF. It turned out that he had the same idea as us and had made a break for it, heading for Menorca before the storms came in.

As darkness fell, we both had to turn our engines on as the wind changed directions and came right on our bow. After an hour or two, we started to see lightning about ten miles in front of us.

I wasn't too worried. I thought I had plenty of sea to skirt around the lighting, but the wind blowing on our bow took the lightning towards us. We quickly put on our heavy weather gear and made sure all the hatches and portholes were closed.

As we headed into the lightning, I assured Mary that we would just pass under the lighting and come out the other side.

"We'll be okay," I told her.

Inside, I was saying my prayers, because as we approached the lightning, the sea became very turbulent. I tried calling Taloa on the VHF, but got no answer — he either couldn't hear me or was too busy battling the elements himself.

The wind was now up to around 35 knots. We had no real options. We could turn back or try and race through it, hoping these were just some squalls and that it would be safe on the other side.

Watching the AIS and radar, Taloa was just ploughing

on forward. I could see his stern lights ahead of me. The radar was now telling me that this was more than just a few squalls. The whole island of Menorca was getting battered by the storm. The storm wasn't supposed to be there for another twelve hours or so.

I couldn't see Taloa's lights now, as visibility was down to just about 100 yards. The noise of the rain battering off the boat was deafening. I told Mary to go down below. There was no reason that both of us needed to get soaked.

I tried to steer the boat portside away from where I thought the worst of the storm was. This went on for a few hours. We were now probably about fifteen miles from Menorca.

It's times like these that you talk about in the pub afterwards, but right at the moment, that's exactly where I wish we were. We had both engines on, but with the wind blowing over 30 knots right onto our bow, we were hardly moving.

"What else can I do?" I thought. There was nothing I could do. The storms that were due tomorrow came twelve hours early. All we could do was say a prayer and push on into the darkness.

Every now and then, I caught a glimpse of Taloa's stern light as our boat lifted out of the water on a wave. Seeing his light gave me some comfort. After what seemed a lifetime, but was only a few hours, we started to see the lights of Menorca.

It was also around this point that we heard a weather warning from the Spanish Coast Guard about heavy weather and storms around Menorca and the Balearic Islands. I wish we'd heard that warning earlier.

As we approached the island, it was hard to make out the entrance to Mahon Marina. This was where we had decided was the safest port. Sometimes, at night, the darkness plays tricks on your eyes. After straining and concentrating for about six hours through the storm, some rocks that I thought were hundreds of feet away were in fact only feet away.

I decided to forget trying to make my way into Mahon using my eyes. Instead, I used the chart plotter to see the true distances of the rocks and other obstacles in our way. The storm was still raging around us, but I just ignored everything and concentrated on the chart plotter, occasionally lifting my head to see over the helm station.

Very quickly, the port and starboard lights of the harbour entrance appeared in front of me. I started to relax. Mary stood at the front of the boat guiding me as we made our way along the long entrance to the port.

Overhead, the storm started to move away from the island. It stopped raining. We couldn't believe it. We had just arrived safe and sound in the harbour, and the bloody storm had moved offshore.

Our hearts were still pounding, and we searched for somewhere to anchor or tie up in the port. The port was full

"Over there, Mary!: I shouted. "There's loads of berths."

"No!" She shouted back. "It doesn't look right."

I didn't care, I wanted off the boat. I wanted a cup of hot tea. So I moored alongside the harbour wall. We tied up the boat and made it safe, and Mary put the kettle on.

"Wow, that was some storm!" We laughed and talked about what we were both thinking. We then climbed into bed for some well-deserved sleep.

In what seemed like five minutes, but was in fact six hrs, there was some loud banging on the hull of the boat. I thought I was dreaming.

"There's someone outside!" Mary yelled.

I climbed out of the berth and went upstairs. There were four army guys there and a woman. She must have seen the Irish Tricolor on the back of the boat because she spoke in English.

"You're moored in a military establishment," she told me. "Move it now!"

We started the engines and untied the boat. In the light, we could see the harbour properly. Last night, it was just a haze of lights when we arrived.

The harbour in Mahon was very long, and we slowly made our way along the length of the channel, checking the place out. It was packed solid with boats. No way would we get berthed anywhere here, so I checked the weather and the chart plotter and found a secluded bay in a nature park about ten miles north. Once out of the harbour, we hoisted the sails and made our way up the coast to a place called Cala De Addaya.

This was a very secluded anchorage in a national park. We dropped anchor and just chilled out. We couldn't get last night's adventure out of our minds. We stayed anchored here for a week. It was great! We walked on the many trails around the park as we waited for our friend Steve Upson to join us.

Steve was making the passage across the Atlantic with us and had managed to find a free week in his calendar before he joined us in Gibraltar in January. He decided to join us for a week on the leg between Menorca and Majorca.

We picked Steve up from the airport a week later, and after provisioning the boat, we sailed up the west coast of Menorca looking for a safe anchorage for the night before sailing across to Majorca.

Eventually, we thought we had found a safe bay for the night. It was a tight bay, but we thought it would be okay, so we dropped the anchor and had a few beers. The beach was only about 100 feet away, so we went ashore for dinner and another few beers.

Later that night, Steve woke us both up in a hurry, he had stayed up on anchor watch when we returned from dinner. The wind was now changing direction, and we were being washed up almost onto the beach. We were all hands on deck and managed to just get the boat far enough away from the beach to turn the engines on and steer away from danger.

It was about three in the morning now. I suggested that we put the sails up and carry on over to Majorca. What we didn't realize was that in all the confusion, somehow our dinghy that we used for getting ashore had become detached from the boat. Mary only noticed this when we were about two miles offshore, so we turned the boat around and circled around the entrance to the bay to see if we could see the dinghy and motor.

It was just too dark, so we waited until first light. Sure enough, there was the dinghy bobbing away at the entrance to the bay. After attaching it to the back of the boat, we hoisted the sails again and headed for Majorca.

It was a fairly uneventful sail from Menorca to Majorca. We arrived late in the afternoon and looked for a secure bay to drop the anchor. We eventually decided on a place called Porto Petro. We hooked onto a mooring ball here for the night, but ended up staying a few days, as the local bar was showing the Rugby World Cup Final on Saturday morning, and Steve was a big England rugby supporter and was determined not to miss it.

The morning after the rugby final, a disappointed Steve suggested that we make our way around the island to the main port of Palma about 35 miles away.

So we hoisted the sails and off we went. After about four hours of sailing with the wind on our beam, the winds changed. Now, they were blowing right on our bow. We couldn't believe our luck. We couldn't make much headway and decided to forget Palma and find a safe bay to drop the anchor. There was nothing really suitable along that part of the coast, and so we decided to head back to Porto Petro.

Over the next few days, the weather never changed. A constant easterly wind blew right onto our nose. So we had to stay in this port for another week before we got any sort of weather window.

In the meantime, Steve had to return to London, so we hired a car and dropped Steve off at the airport. Our plan was to meet him again in Gibraltar in January. So for the next few days, Mary and I drove all around the island sightseeing. We hadn't realized how big the island was, and it was great to see, but we were desperate to get moving again. It was now the 8th of November, and we needed to be in Gibraltar before Christmas. The wind was still against us, but we saw a small break in the weather and decided to make a run for it to Ibiza 75 miles away. If the weather held, hopefully we could make it to Cartagena on the Spanish mainland 200 miles away.

It wasn't ideal conditions to leave that morning, but we had been holed up in Porto Petro for over a week now, and I figured the gamble was worth it.

That was my first big mistake. In future, I will not let my impatience get the better of me. If I have to wait a month in port for the right weather, then I will. We were about to learn a lesson the hard way.

Almost as soon as we were outside the bay, the sea was against us. The clear blue skies above us were very deceptive. If you were looking out to sea from land, it looked like a beautiful day. Maybe just a bit windy. But down on the water, it was a different matter.

Our weather forecast indicated the wind would be coming from the north for 5-6 hours. This was what I had based my plans on. It would give us a nice beam reach sail to Ibiza. But the wind was right on the nose again. I dropped the sails and decided to motor all the way to Ibiza.

All went well for a few hours. Then the seas started to build. The blue skies were now a distant memory. The waves started to build to nearly three meters high. We were starting to get battered. It felt like we were inside a washing machine. Mary and I already had the heavy weather gear on, and we were tied to the boat by a lifeline each. This was the second time this had happened to us in two weeks.

During our 2016 voyage, we had never experienced weather like we had since we left Malta about seven weeks earlier. I kept asking myself if I was making bad judgement calls or if we were just unlucky. I knew from different old sailors that the Mediterranean can be really unpredictable in the winter. But I was studying the weather and the forecasts. We were downloading forecasts hourly, but I still wasn't getting it right.

Anyway, we ploughed on. The waves were crashing right over the boat now, and the rigging was taking a real battering. I started to look at my options. There was nothing I could think to do — only turn the boat around and go with the waves instead of fighting them. It was dark now, and it felt like we were on a roller coaster.

I thought of those old boys who caught the crab out on the Bering Sea. Maybe I was overreacting. I decided to carry on.

We tried to eat some stew that I had made before we left, but that was impossible. The boat was moving violently up and down the waves, and just trying to steer at the helm and eat was impossible. Mary also took her turn at the helm, but neither of us could eat anything. This went on for hours through the night.

Soon enough, we saw the sun rising behind us. That lifted the spirits for a while. I was worried about damage to the boat and kept checking the rigging as best we could. Everything seemed okay. Since we had left Majorca the morning before, we hadn't seen any other boats, not even fishermen. That should have been a clue to me. I swore to myself that I would never take a chance and get caught like this again.

Far off in the distance, we could now see the cliffs of Ibiza. We were about fifteen miles out. Another 4-5 hours, and we would be out of the washing machine.

All that afternoon, the wind and the waves never let up. In a strange way, we were starting to get used to the battering. It was dusk now, and the lights on land were starting to come on. There was no chance of getting into a port in daylight now.

We headed for the port of Santa Eulalia. Usually, I would look for an anchorage — you didn't have to pay for that. But there was no way I wanted to anchor out tonight, and it must have been around 8 pm when we limped into Santa Eulalia. It was Saturday night, and Ibiza being the place it was, there was music coming from all the bars around the marina. Lots of people around were enjoying themselves.

None of it interested us. We just wanted a good feed and a night's sleep.

Next morning, we checked the boat over. Surprisingly, it was in good shape externally. Inside, everything had been thrown everywhere. But that was easily fixed. We had breakfast and Googled the nearest chapel to go to Mass. It was only round the corner, so Mary and I just sat there for about an hour. We thanked God for helping us make it safely to shore.

After a few days' rest, and after checking the weather, we decided to sail around the southern part of Ibiza and round the western coast to a little bay called Porroig. From here, it was a 60-mile sail straight to the mainland and a place called Calpe.

We could have sailed the 400 miles straight to Gibraltar from Ibiza, but thought we would day hop it along the Spanish Coast and enjoy the views. Late that afternoon, as we approached the small bay of Porroig, I noticed that the bay was a lot smaller than it appeared on the charts. Our 41-foot boat would be too big for the bay, and with the northerly winds forecast that night, we needed to stay in that general area to give us the shelter that we needed. We had a look around at other bays, but came back to Porroig.

Now it was just before dark. There was a mooring ball near the centre of the bay. I told Mary we would hook onto that for the night. This was something that we had done hundreds of times before. As I approached the mooring ball, I cut the engines.

Mary stretched out with her long wooden pole and hook to attach a line, but with the wind catching the side of the boat, it started to blow us off the mooring ball. Mary tried to hold the pole and hook, but the pressure of the boat moving away from the mooring ball in the wind was taking the pole from her hand. If we lost the pole and hook we were in trouble.

So I rushed from the helm station and quickly grabbed the pole, pulling on the hook with all my strength. I felt the pressure lightening. Then, the wind started to take the boat away from the mooring ball, and as I grabbed hold of the pole and hook, the mooring ball rope pulled me against the safety railing on the boat.

I heard my ribs crack. It was agony, but I couldn't let go.

"Mary, I think I just broke something!" I shouted.

Mary pulled the pole with me, and we managed to attach our rope to the mooring ball. We secured the boat properly against the mooring ball and went below.

I was doubled over. I told Mary that I heard something break. As usual, she told me to "suck it up." I could hardly get into bed. The pain was excruciating. But what could we do? We were in the dark in a small bay with no one around for miles.

I lay on the bed that night with my clothes on, hoping I didn't have to use the toilet during the night. Every movement hurt like hell. Our original plan was to leave at 5 am to ensure that we arrived in Calpe the next day before dark.

The next morning, I struggled to wiggle my way out of the bed. Even brushing my teeth was an ordeal, but I got up. We went through our safety procedures before starting the engines and undoing our lines from the mooring ball.

We were off towards the mainland. It was still dark, but that night was a full moon, and we followed the light from the moon across the water out of the bay and headed for Calpe.

That day would've usually been a normal day's sailing, but every movement of the boat was bloody painful, and we had another twelve hours of it. Mary took the helm as I lay in the main saloon, but this didn't really help. In fact, it was better to stand up than lie down.

"Suck it up! Mary would shout at me.

I think it was our upbringing. We had both been brought up in Belfast, where you got no sympathy. My Da would shout, "Get on with it!" if we complained about anything, and Mary's da was the same. So I just had to suck it up and hope we reached land soon.

It was around 7 pm and dark when we eventually arrived in Calpe. The massive rock at the harbour entrance was called the Peñón de Ifach. It rose nearly 350 meters high. We had seen it nearly twenty miles out at sea.

The harbour was at the bottom of the rock. I tried to find a berth in the harbour, but it was full, and the private marina was also full. I spotted a small concrete wall in part of the commercial part of the harbour and tied up there. I told Mary we would sort it out in the morning with the harbour master.

The next morning, we went to the main office. No one was about.

"We'll come back later," I told Mary. "I need to get to the hospital."

We found a taxi and headed to the local hospital. Luckily, we didn't have to wait long. The nurse took me straight into the x-ray room. We waited in the waiting room for the results. Not long after, the nurse returned.

"You've broken some ribs," She said. "There's more damage there. I want you to go to the main hospital at Dénia. It's about twenty miles away."

So we had to get another taxi. The journey in the cab was excruciating. I felt every bump in the road, but eventually we arrived. After a seven-hour wait, they took me into the x-ray room again. The result was one broken rib and two fractured ribs.

I looked at Mary as if to say, "I told you so." "Suck it up, mister!" Was all I got back.

The doctor told us to rest completely and come back in two weeks. We both knew there was no chance of that. After the storms and bad weather we had experienced — and now this — I really thought the gods were against us.

After a week of doing nothing and looking at four bare walls, we were both desperate to get going again. I kept checking the weather a few times a day, but the soreness and acute pain from the broken ribs had left me doubled up like an old man. I thought that if we could get back out to sea again, things would get better. The next port I was looking at was Cartagena.

This historic naval port was about 80 nautical miles down the Costa Brava. It would mean an overnight sail, but if we had calm seas, it would be a doddle on the ribs. I suggested to Mary that we go on the next northerly wind, which was due in 24 hours.

Sure enough, the next morning, the winds were blowing in the right direction, and we left Calpe early after breakfast.

It was a beautiful, sunny day. As we sailed away from the shore, I made my way out to about ten miles offshore. This is something that we always do because it takes us out of the way of the jet skis, power boat posers, and fishermen's lobster pots that litter the coasts of the Med. Out here, we had none of those obstacles, and we could get all the sails up, including our spinnaker.

I stayed at the helm most of the time, and Mary did all the heavy lifting and adjusting the sails. We could see Benidorm and Alicante off to our right as we sailed down the coast. It was just starting to get dark as we passed Torrevieja.

We decided to drop all the sails in case there were any problems during the night. We just unfurled our small genoa and motor sailed the rest of the night. There is nothing quite like night sailing especially, if you have a calm sea and a cloudless sky. Once offshore and away from any light pollution, the sky and the stars just seem so vast and far away. Many nights, we've seen shooting stars flying across the sky, and also some other things that are just too hard to explain.

If we can, we try to coordinate night passages with a full moon. The natural light the moon gives across the water is just brilliant. The full moon also gives a sense of security, because it is not natural to just sail into the darkness, especially in heavy weather.

It was a quiet night,. and we arrived safely in Cartagena around 3 am and tied the boat up against the marina pontoon. In the morning, after registering with the marine office, the carpintería helped us moor the boat properly, as I couldn't lift or pull any ropes because of my ribs.

Cartagena is an old Roman port, and the Romans had

been sailing in and out since 220BC. There were some unbelievable old Roman ruins with a magnificent amphitheatre in the centre of town.

After we had been in port a few days our old friend Taloa — the boat that was in the storm with us back in Menorca — came into port. Her owner and his wife came over to find us. They had been really battered in the storm as well, and it turned out that they had been following us on the AIS for a few weeks now and had stopped in all the same places as us. They explained that they would not night sail again. I think the experience that night had a big effect on them.

I explained that we were thinking of leaving in the next day or so heading down the coast to Almerimar depending on the weather. They said they would follow us down there.

We also met Charlie and Sue Buehler in Cartagena. They had a catamaran like us, and we had met them around Easter back in Malta when they anchored in the bay where we lived. Charlie and Sue were Canadian, and their boat was called Purrr. They intended to sail across the Atlantic at the same time as us, and we had a lot in common with them. They are a great couple, and Charlie was very helpful to us with sailing and boating information and tips.

They invited us and some others onto their boat one night for a few drinks and dinner. It turned out that most of the people there that night were all making the Atlantic crossing. Charlie left Cartagena the next morning, and we followed his course on the AIS as he made his way across the Atlantic. He arrived in Saint Lucia in January 2020

The sail from Cartagena to Almerimar was around 120 miles, which meant another overnight sail or 4-5 days of coast hopping. I waited for a good weather window and prepared the boat. We decided to sail at night.

It turned out to be a great move, and we had a fantastic sail down to Alimermar. Mary still had to do all the heavy work and adjust the sails on the way. During the night, we had a near miss with a fishing boat that was trawling without any lights on, but we had become used to the unusual happening during the night at sea. You just had to be aware at all times, and I was always checking the radar every day for obstacles.

We arrived safely the next day in Almerimar. After tying up in the marina, we checked for Taloa to see how they were getting on. But they decided to day hop instead of the night sailing, and it took them four days to arrive in Almerimar.

Since we had left Malta back in September, I had kept in touch with friends and family through our Iridium Go WIFi setup on the boat. This allowed us to make phone calls offshore and download the weather on an hourly basis. Mary could keep in touch with her family through Facebook. My Da, who had not been well for a while, was also taken back into hospital during this trip, and the family had set up a WhatsApp group so that everyone could be kept informed about what was going on with him. I thought this was a great tool, as we were getting daily updates on the old man.

Just as we arrived in Almerimar, my Da took a turn for the worse and was moved to a high-dependency room. The prognosis was not great. I told Mary that we needed to go back to the UK. We could leave the boat in the marina here and get a flight locally to Madrid and onto Gatwick.

The next day, we were on our way to the UK

By this time, I was having serious thoughts about our whole Atlantic crossing. I had been planning this trip for eighteen months and spent a small fortune getting the boat ready for the trip.

But since we left Malta, it felt that the trip was jinxed. We had experienced storms like we never had before. I'd broken my ribs. My Da's health had taken a turn for the worse.

"What else could go wrong?" I thought.

I mentioned to Mary my thoughts and concerns. At the time, we were having a new house being built for us in Florida. In fact, it was almost ready to move into. Our original plan had been to sail across the Atlantic and back to the Mediterranean, leave the boat back in Malta, and fly over to Florida to live there. Now, I was having second thoughts about the crossing.

I suggested to Mary that we go to the UK to see my Da and see how it worked out. We could then take a flight to Florida and leave the boat in Almerimar. We could always come back to the boat next year.

"Yes, let's do that." she said.

When we arrived in the UK, we went straight to the hospital. The old man was not in great shape. He had lost a lot of weight since that last time we had seen him a few months earlier. But he recognised us and gave me a thumbs up.

I left the hospital that night and knew it was only a matter of time. The next morning, my sister Maria rang me.

"The hospital's been in touch," she said. "Can you go straight there and ask for Dr Helen.

When I got there, the doctor called me into a private room and told me that the old man didn't have long to live.

"How long?" I asked, but she just shrugged her shoulders.

She told me that I should contact all the family and that they should come to say their goodbyes.

"I want to explain this again, but in front of your dad, so that he understands what's happening," she said.

As we walked towards his bed, it felt so surreal. The doctor didn't mince her words and explained to the old man what was going to happen. She asked again if we had any questions.

I looked at the old man.

"Do you understand what she just said?"

He sort of nodded. I welled up inside.

Not knowing what to do or say, the doctor left us. I grabbed the old man's hand and whispered in his ear and sat there in shock.

After a while, he nodded off to sleep, and I phoned my brothers and sisters and explained to them what the doctor had told me. Everyone came straight to the hospital, including grandkids. There were just too many people at the hospital that night, so we decided that we would put a shift routine into place so that there was always someone with him all the time. Everyone played their part.

Nine days later, the old man died. What a shock. Even though we knew it was going to happen, it was still surreal when Seamus, my brother, rang to tell us the news.

The Starry Plough, moored in Malta, just leaving for the Atlantic

24 | FAMILY AND REFLECTIONS

This book has been a great voyage of reflection. Although there have been plenty of ups and downs in my life, I don't regret too much.

Now, as I can look back over the trials and tribulations, I would ask people who think their futures are bleak to stop and ask themselves a question: If yer man can do it, why can't I?

It's all about work ethic. It seemed to me the harder, I worked, the luckier I got. I always took every opportunity. Sometimes, it led me down to a dead end. But other times, it opened doors that I ran through. Taking opportunities took me from a man with a wheelbarrow to running multimillion-pound companies.

Education wasn't the path for me. All I had were my hands and mouth and a great ambition. In later years, I learned how much education really matters and how much I must have missed from bunking off school all those times. Now, I am always looking for new ways of learning. Over the years, I've attended so many different night classes for so many different things. I am as hungry as ever to learn new things. Like they say, "you don't know what you don't know."

My greatest achievement though is not my businesses or my adventures. It's my two daughters, Faye and Sinead. I may not have been there all the time when they were growing up, since I was always working. And they may not always have seen eye-to-eye with me. But I can't help being so proud of them both and how they've turned out.

My Ma and Da brought us up to show respect, have manners, help others, look after each other, and have a good work ethic. I'm glad to have these virtues. I'm even happier that both Faye and Sinead have these same values. Although they've been privileged in some ways, they were brought up to know the value of a pound coin. If they wanted anything, they had to work for it.

When Faye left school, she was in a dead-end job at Gatwick just to earn her own money. She then put herself through university as a quantity surveyor. She kept going and finished as a chartered surveyor, being the only female in the class. Out on site couldn't have been easy, but she finished university with top grades.

Instead of coming straight into our business, I suggested that she go out into the real world and learn from her mistakes at other people's expense. In a few years' time, she could come back to the family firm. She did this and more. Now, she is married to Sybe. They have two great kids, Roman and Raine. We set up a property development business between us that is managed on a daily basis by Faye and Sybe. It's going from strength to strength.

Sinead is at the centre of everything in our main business. As a qualified accountant, she handles the company finances. She doesn't miss much. She has a great appetite for work. It's not unusual to find her in front of a computer screen long after office hours. A few years ago, she and Barrie Rossiter were promoted to directors. They take this role very seriously and have come up with some great ideas. They are the future of the business.

In 2018, Sinead got married to Harriet. What a day that was! Harriet is also our company's buyer, and these two are a great team in and out of work.

Hopefully, you've enjoyed reading this book. I wanted to put the record straight on a few things which I have done, and perhaps if even a single young person learns something from these pages, then it's all been worth it.

All the proceeds from this book are going to The Open House, a charity in Crawley for the homeless, they operate with very little overheads so all monies will go directly to helping those without their own roof.

Thank you.

My two daughters, Sinead & Faye

Faye getting her degree as a chartered quantity surveyor

Leonard Nugent

My two grandsons, Roman & Raine, they would eat the hands off ye

Sinead & Harriet on their wedding day

Printed in Great Britain
by Amazon